SHEBEEN

A Play in Three Acts

by Mufaro Makubika

samuelfrench.co.uk

Cover artwork designed by Gemma Leggett.

THINKING ABOUT PERFORMING A SHOW?

There are thousands of plays and musicals available to perform from Samuel French right now, and applying for a licence is easier and more affordable than you might think

From classic plays to brand new musicals, from monologues to epic dramas, there are shows for everyone.

Plays and musicals are protected by copyright law so if you want to perform them, the first thing you'll need is a licence. This simple process helps support the playwright by ensuring they get paid for their work, and means that you'll have the documents you need to stage the show in public.

Not all our shows are available to perform all the time, so it's important to check and apply for a licence before you start rehearsals or commit to doing the show.

LEARN MORE & FIND THOUSANDS OF SHOWS

Browse our full range of plays and musicals and find out more about how to license a show

www.samuelfrench.co.uk/perform

Talk to the friendly experts in our Licensing team for advice on choosing a show, and help with licensing

plays@samuelfrench.co.uk   020 7387 9373

Acting Editions

BORN TO PERFORM

Playscripts designed from the ground up to work the way you do in rehearsal, performance and study

---

Larger, clearer text for easier reading

Wider margins for notes

Performance features such as character and props lists, sound and lighting cues, and more

---

+ CHOOSE A SIZE AND STYLE TO SUIT YOU

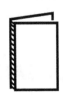

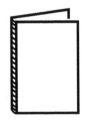

STANDARD EDITION

Our regular paperback book at our regular size

SPIRAL-BOUND EDITION

The same size as the Standard Edition, but with a sturdy, easy-to-fold, easy-to-hold spiral-bound spine

LARGE EDITION

A4 size and spiral bound, with larger text and a blank page for notes opposite every page of text. Perfect for technical and directing use

---

LEARN MORE | **samuelfrench.co.uk/actingeditions**

Nottingham Playhouse

Nottingham Playhouse is a leading UK producing theatre. Since 1948 we have been creating bold and imaginative productions, both large and small: timeless classics, enthralling family shows and adventurous new commissions, touring work nationally and internationally.

Notable recent productions include widely-acclaimed miner's strike play *Wonderland* by award-winning writer Beth Steel; Louis Sachar's family drama, *Holes*; Robert Icke's *1984*, which has enjoyed two West-End runs, international tours and a transfer to Broadway; a major revival of *Touched* starring BAFTA winning actress Vicky McClure, and the European premiere production of *The Kite Runner* which has had major success in the West End and three national tours.

2018 highlights includes the Broadway musical *Sweet Charity* and *The Madness of George III* which stars Mark Gatiss.

★ ★ ★ ★ ★ "Blazing with clinical, spine-tingling finesse"
The Telegraph (on *1984*)

★ ★ ★ ★ "This is a big play, ambitious in the way it melds the public and the private, full of heart and very little sentimentality"
The Guardian (on *Wonderland*)

★ ★ ★ ★ "It's a show that grows in pace, wit and emotional resonance the more it goes on; you'll leave smiling"
The Times (on *Holes*)

★ ★ ★ ★ "Stands shoulder to shoulder with the best ... a hit."
The Telegraph (on *The Kite Runner*)

Chief Executive: Stephanie Sirr
Artistic Director: Adam Penford

ABOUT THE AUTHOR

Mufaro Makubika is a playwright who lives and works in Nottingham. Credits for Nottingham Playhouse: *How To Breathe.*

Shebeen was the winner of the 2017 Alfred Fagon Award for best new play.

MUSIC USE NOTE

Licensees are solely responsible for obtaining formal written permission from copyright owners to use copyrighted music in the performance of this play and are strongly cautioned to do so. If no such permission is obtained by the licensee, then the licensee must use only original music that the licensee owns and controls. Licensees are solely responsible and liable for all music clearances and shall indemnify the copyright owners of the play(s) and their licensing agent, Samuel French, against any costs, expenses, losses and liabilities arising from the use of music by licensees. Please contact the appropriate music licensing authority in your territory for the rights to any incidental music.

USE OF COPYRIGHT MUSIC

A licence issued by Samuel French Ltd to perform this play does not include permission to use the incidental music specified in this copy.

Where the place of performance is already licensed by the PERFORMING RIGHT SOCIETY (PRS) a return of the music used must be made to them. If the place of performance is not so licensed then application should be made to the PRS, 2 Pancras Square, London, N1C 4AG.

A separate and additional licence from
PHONOGRAPHIC PERFORMANCE LTD,
1 Upper James Street, London W1F 9DE (www.ppluk.com)
is needed whenever commercial recordings are used.

IMPORTANT BILLING AND CREDIT REQUIREMENTS

If you have obtained performance rights to this title, please refer to your licensing agreement for important billing and credit requirements.

Shebeen, by Mufaro Makubika, commissioned by Nottingham Playhouse was first performed by Nottingham Playhouse Theatre Company, in association with Theatre Royal Stratford East, at Nottingham Playhouse on 1 June 2018, with the following cast and creative team:

GEORGE	Karl Collins
PEARL	Martina Laird
EARNEST	Rolan Bell
MRS CLARK	Hazel Ellerby
MARY	Chloe Harris
SARGEANT WILLIAMS	Karl Haynes
CONSTABLE REED / ROBERT DUNNE	Adam Rojko Vega
LINFORD	Theo Solomon
GAYLE	Danielle Walters

Director	Matthew Xia
Designer	Grace Smart
Lighting Designer	Ciarán Cunningham
Sound Designer / Composer	Richard Hammarton
Movement Director	Rachael Nanyonjo
Fight Director	Kev McCurdy
Dialect Coach	Hazel Holder
Dramaturg	Kirsty Patrick Ward
Casting Director	Sarah Bird CDG
Casting Director	Sophie Parrott CDG

CHARACTERS

PEARL – Female, black, late thirties, Jamaican living in district around the St Ann's Well Road.

GEORGE – Male, black, early forties, Pearl's husband, Jamaican living in the district St Ann's Well Road.

EARNEST – Male, black, thirties, Trinidadian immigrant living in district around the St Ann's Well Road.

LINFORD – Male, black, early twenties, Jamaican immigrant living in the district around the St Ann's Well Road.

MARY – Female, white, early twenties, born and living in the district around the St Ann's Well Road.

GAYLE – Female, black, twenties, Jamaican immigrant living in the district around the St Ann's Well Road.

MRS CLARK – Female, white, late forties to early fifties, a neighbour, Mary's mother. Nottingham born and living in the district around the St Ann's Well Road.

SARGEANT WILLIAMS – Male, white, late forties, police officer. Nottingham born and living in the district around the St Ann's Well Road.

CONSTABLE REED – Male, white, Mid- to late twenties, Nottingham born.

ROBERT DUNNE – Male, white, twenties, London born.

Supernumeraries to play the GUESTS.

The actor who plays CONSTANBLE REED also plays ROBERT DUNNE

SETTING

August 1958.

The district around the St Ann's Well Road, Nottingham.

A home.

A green carpet. Brown and green wallpaper with elaborate designs of birds. In the corner is one of those displays cabinets with a sliding glass doors packed full of crockery and glasses which only come out on special occasions. On a little doyley wrapped coffee table in the middle is a very bright purple vase full of artificial flowers. There are a lot of doilies in the room. In the corner, a pristine and shiny looking gold drinks tray laden with all sorts of rums and liquors. In one corner is a heating lamp which has blackened the ceiling right above it. Some of the wallpaper is peeling off. Pictures on the wall of George and Pearl. George in his trunks and gloves. There is also a picture of a young Queen Elizabeth II. She looks out at us. Doors leading off to the kitchen and the rest of the house.

AUTHOR'S NOTE

/ represents an interruption.
Stage directions are in italics.
Dialogue in between ... are private conversations in public.
Unspoken thoughts/intentions are in brackets.
Song choices are suggestions.

THANKS TO

Esther Richardson, Fiona Buffini, Giles Croft,
Adam Penford, Stephanie Sirr, Kirsty Patrick Ward,
Matthew Xia, Nick Quinn
and the community of St Ann's, Nottingham.

For Janet

ACT ONE

Early Saturday evening. PEARL's cleaning and cooking.
PEARL wipes the glass doors on a display cabinet.
PEARL's clear and focused.
At the end of the act, the home is a shebeen.
A knock at the door from outside.

PEARL Who is it?

SERGEANT WILLIAMS Mrs Brown?

Beat.

PEARL You going to say what you want?

SERGEANT WILLIAMS Sergeant Williams.

PEARL Who?

SERGEANT WILLIAMS The police.

PEARL takes her time.
PEARL opens the door.

PEARL Didn't recognise your voice, through the door.
Come in.

SERGEANT WILLIAMS You weren't to know.

SERGEANT WILLIAMS stands at the door.

PEARL Please come in.

SERGEANT WILLIAMS wipes his shoes on a mat.
SERGEANT WILLIAMS takes off his hat and mops his brow.

SERGEANT WILLIAMS *comes in.*

SERGEANT WILLIAMS Thank you.

PEARL How can I help you officer?

SERGEANT WILLIAMS Is Mr Brown around?

PEARL He gone shop.

SERGEANT WILLIAMS Do you think Mr Brown will be back soon?

PEARL What do you want with George?

SERGEANT WILLIAMS I was hoping to speak to Mr Brown, madam.
An official matter.

PEARL He in trouble officer?

SERGEANT WILLIAMS Do you know when he'll be back?

PEARL Can I help?

SERGEANT WILLIAMS I'd need to speak to him personally.

PEARL You're starting to scare me officer.

SERGEANT WILLIAMS Don't be alarmed.
I just need to speak to Mr Brown that's all.
A courtesy call if you like.

PEARL He soon back.
Me expecting him soon.

SERGEANT WILLIAMS I'll come back later.
Thank you.

SERGEANT WILLIAMS *about to leave.*

PEARL Stay.
No need to go.
Mr Brown.
George, is on his way.

SERGEANT WILLIAMS I can wait outside.

PEARL Don't need to.

Nice and cool in here.

Sit.

SERGEANT WILLIAMS You sure, madam?

That Mr Brown won't mind.

PEARL I don't mind.

SERGEANT WILLIAMS I don't think that's a good idea.

PEARL Why?

SERGEANT WILLIAMS Why?

PEARL Yes, why?

Beat.

SERGEANT WILLIAMS You are a woman alone in her home.

Your husband isn't here.

PEARL This my home as well Sergeant.

I've asked you to stay.

SERGEANT WILLIAMS *unsure.*

Sit.

SERGEANT WILLIAMS I can stand.

PEARL You can sit if you want.

SERGEANT WILLIAMS I'll stand.

PEARL Suit yourself.

SERGEANT WILLIAMS *stands.*

Don't mind if I work while you wait?

SERGEANT WILLIAMS A woman's work is never done, right?

PEARL That's true.

PEARL *exits into the kitchen to check on her cooking.*

SERGEANT WILLIAMS *stands and wait.*

SERGEANT WILLIAMS *looks around the room.*

PEARL *returns.*

Would you like a drink officer?

Tea?

Beat.

Something stronger?

SERGEANT WILLIAMS I'm alright, thank you Mrs Brown.

PEARL Pearl.

Beat.

SERGEANT WILLIAMS Right.

PEARL Don't think we've been properly introduced.
Say hello on the street.
That's all.

Beat.

Yours?

SERGEANT WILLIAMS Like I said before, Sergeant Williams
will do.

Silence.

I can come back later.

PEARL Relax Sergeant Williams.
He soon back.

PEARL *continues cleaning the display cabinet.*

SERGEANT WILLIAMS *waits.*

PEARL *wipes the glass doors down with a wet cloth.*

PEARL *dries the glass doors with newspaper.*

PEARL *moves on to the drinks tray.*

PEARL *wipes down each spirit bottle with a wet cloth.*

PEARL *wipes down the frame of the display cabinet.*

SERGEANT WILLIAMS That smells great.

PEARL Sorry?

SERGEANT WILLIAMS What you are cooking.
It smells great.

PEARL Thank you.

Pause.

SERGEANT WILLIAMS What is it?
What you are cooking?

PEARL Curried mutton.

Beat.

Would you like some Sergeant?

SERGEANT WILLIAMS No I'm fine, thank you.
I have tea waiting for me at home.

PEARL Your wife cook curried mutton too?

SERGEANT WILLIAMS Not quite curried mutton.
She wouldn't know how to.

Beat.

I need to save myself for me tea.

PEARL What are you having?
She cook good for you?

SERGEANT WILLIAMS Maybe egg and chips.
I don't know.

Beat.

PEARL You must have some mutton then.
You like chips and egg?

SERGEANT WILLIAMS It suits me fine.
I eat whatever she makes.

She's my wife.

Beat.

PEARL Won't you sit officer?

Please.

Pause.

SERGEANT WILLIAMS Only for a bit.

SERGEANT WILLIAMS *looks at the picture of* GEORGE
on the wall.

PEARL *notices* SERGEANT WILLIAMS *looking.*

I've heard about Mr Brown.

PEARL You seen him fight?

SERGEANT WILLIAMS No.

Heard he was a good fighter though.

PEARL A great fighter once.

Not anymore.

Silence.

SERGEANT WILLIAMS The wallpaper.

Mine comes off too. .

It's these old houses.

Get the damp/

PEARL It's the best we can get.

SERGEANT WILLIAMS I didn't mean anything by that Mrs Brown.

PEARL *gets a bottle of rum and two glasses from the*
drinks tray.

PEARL I'm going to have a little drink.

Would you like to join me?

SERGEANT WILLIAMS I'm working.

Thank you though.

PEARL Look like a man who's had a long hard day.

Beat.

Tried Jamaican rum?

SERGEANT WILLIAMS I can't say I have.

PEARL This here.

This rum make you feel good.

SERGEANT WILLIAMS I'm on the job.

PEARL So am I, Sergeant Williams.

PEARL *laughs.*

You going to let me drink on me own?

Just a sip.

Refused my food.

Now you refusing my drink.

SERGEANT WILLIAMS *unsure.*

We'll keep it between us.

Just a taste.

PEARL *pours two glasses of rum.*

PEARL *passes a glass of rum to* SERGEANT WILLIAMS.

SERGEANT WILLIAMS *reluctantly accepts.*

SERGEANT WILLIAMS I really shouldn't.

PEARL It's just rum.

What could it hurt?

SERGEANT WILLIAMS *stares at the rum unsure.*

Fighting the urge to drink.

Go on.

Take that down.

Make you feel good.

PEARL *drinks.*

SERGEANT WILLIAMS *drinks.*

That make you feel good?

SERGEANT WILLIAMS It's nice, thank you.

SERGEANT WILLIAMS *drains his glass.*

PEARL You know how to drink.
I like that.

Beat.

Do you mind if I play some music?
While you wait.

SERGEANT WILLIAMS Not at all.

PEARL *puts on a record.*
"LONDON IS THE PLACE FOR ME" by Lord Kitchener.
The song gently plays in the background.
PEARL *continues cleaning the display cabinet.*
SERGEANT WILLIAMS *taps his foot.*
PEARL *notices.*

PEARL You like it?

SERGEANT WILLIAMS I don't mind it.

PEARL Kind of music you dance to.
You dance Sergeant?

SERGEANT WILLIAMS Not much.

PEARL *dances a little.*

PEARL Move your body to the music.

SERGEANT WILLIAMS I couldn't do that.

PEARL *laughs.*

PEARL Would you like another drink?

SERGEANT WILLIAMS I don't think I can.

PEARL Sure you can.

Between us.

You have my word.

Can trust me.

SERGEANT WILLIAMS I don't know.

PEARL One more.

PEARL *pours another glass of rum for* **SERGEANT WILLIAMS.**

PEARL *pours a drink for herself.*

PEARL *hands him the drink.*

SERGEANT WILLIAMS *sips his drink.*

SERGEANT WILLIAMS Thank you.

PEARL *drains her drink.*

For your welcome.

Letting me into your home.

PEARL You welcome.

Like to think we friends now.

Pause.

Can I ask you a question Sergeant?

SERGEANT WILLIAMS If I can answer it.

Beat.

PEARL How long you been with your wife?

If that's not too personal?

Pause.

SERGEANT WILLIAMS Married twenty-eight years.

PEARL Do you have kids?

SERGEANT WILLIAMS Three boys and a girl.

PEARL Two girls.
Vivian and Esther.

SERGEANT WILLIAMS Been together thirty years.
Me and my girl.

PEARL What does it take?

SERGEANT WILLIAMS Sorry?

PEARL To stay together that long?
What does it take?

SERGEANT WILLIAMS I don't know.

PEARL Surely you must.
Marriage is work, right?

SERGEANT WILLIAMS Love.

PEARL Love is important.
Me and George haven't been together that long.
We talk though.
You talk to your wife?

SERGEANT WILLIAMS I do.

PEARL (About) How you feel?
When your feet feel tired.
Partners.
Me and George.
We partners.

Pause.

Tells me how he feels.
Know what he's thinking.
Share everything.
Worry about each other.
Understand?

SERGEANT WILLIAMS Maybe I should go.

PEARL No need.
We are friends now.

Beat.

Why are you here?
What do you want with George?

Pause.

SERGEANT WILLIAMS You have parties here?

PEARL Sorry Sergeant Williams.
Parties.
People.
Music.
Food.

Beat.

Parties.

Pause.

PEARL We have friends over.

SERGEANT WILLIAMS You have a lot of friends.

PEARL We are lucky.

Beat.

SERGEANT WILLIAMS Indeed.
That many friends.

Pause.

I was born here.
I live here.
It's my home/

PEARL And mine.
Home sweet home.

SERGEANT WILLIAMS We are all on top of each other.
Neighbours and that.
We are bursting at the seams.
Criminals running amok.

PEARL Hardworking men and women.

SERGEANT WILLIAMS The thing is I believe in the law.
I'm sworn to serve this community.
You.
I believe in not giving crime a chance to happen.

Beat.

You heard about the attack on the high street?

PEARL Heard something about it.

SERGEANT WILLIAMS Is he one of your friends?

PEARL We all don't know each other Sergeant Williams.

SERGEANT WILLIAMS From what I've heard he's been here.
For a party.

PEARL Maybe in the past.
He doesn't come here anymore.

Pause.

SERGEANT WILLIAMS Now...
With your parties.
I...

Beat.

I just hope there isn't trouble.
You understand?

PEARL Never been trouble before.

SERGEANT WILLIAMS We all turn a blind eye.
I hope we can keep doing that.

Beat.

That you don't cause trouble.

That's what the people here require.

From St Ann's.

That's my job.

Beat.

I'm not saying we are all angels.

There are streets, I wouldn't walk alone at night.

But it's home.

Beat.

You understand?

PEARL Perfectly officer.

> GEORGE *enters from outside carrying beer slung over his shoulder.*
>
> SERGEANT WILLIAMS *stands.*

GEORGE This heat making me sweat.

PEARL George, we have company.

> GEORGE *puts the beer down.*

GEORGE Sergeant, I didn't see you there.

SERGEANT WILLIAMS Mr Brown.

GEORGE Sergeant Williams.

> GEORGE *and* SERGEANT WILLIAMS *shake hands.*

PEARL He came looking for you.
Told him he could wait.

GEORGE Just gone shop sergeant.

PEARL Told him that.

GEORGE My wife look after you?

SERGEANT WILLIAMS She was very kind.

GEORGE *notices the glass of rum.*

SERGEANT WILLIAMS *is embarrassed.*

I was just passing by/

GEORGE How can I help you officer?

SERGEANT WILLIAMS Well/

PEARL There's been trouble around St Ann's.
The sergeant was making sure we were fine.
Weren't you sergeant?

Beat.

SERGEANT WILLIAMS That's right.
Hot summers bring out hot tempers.

Beat.

You've heard about the incident on the Well's Road.
A young coloured chap.
Got his head put through a window.

GEORGE He is a friend.

SERGEANT WILLIAMS He is a friend of yours.
He came to the parties?

PEARL An acquaintance.

GEORGE A friend.

PEARL Doesn't come to parties anymore.

Beat.

We're fine.
Can see yourself.

SERGEANT WILLIAMS *(a look to* **PEARL***)* I see that.

SERGEANT WILLIAMS *notices the beer.*

That for a party tonight?

PEARL Having friends over sergeant.
Have friends over all the time.

Silence.

SERGEANT WILLIAMS I'll be going.
Work waits for no man.

PEARL Or woman.

Beat.

SERGEANT WILLIAMS Right.
All I ask is that you are vigilant tonight.

PEARL We will Sergeant Williams.

SERGEANT WILLIAMS Mark.

GEORGE Sorry.

SERGEANT WILLIAMS My name is Mark.

PEARL Mark.

Beat.

Don't you want to finish your drink Mark?

SERGEANT WILLIAMS *drains the rum.*

SERGEANT WILLIAMS *prepares to leave.*

SERGEANT WILLIAMS *shakes hands with* GEORGE.

SERGEANT WILLIAMS Mr and Mrs Brown.
Thank you.

SERGEANT WILLIAMS *exits.*

GEORGE What's going on here?

PEARL The sergeant came to see if we were alright.

GEORGE Mark?

PEARL We friends now.

GEORGE And the rum?

PEARL Looking after our guest.

GEORGE He's not a guest.
He's police.

PEARL We don't have to worry about that.

GEORGE He knows about the shebeen/

PEARL We don't have to worry about him.
Trust me.

GEORGE We shouldn't open tonight.

PEARL Why?

GEORGE Until things calm down.
Michael's in hospital.

PEARL When was the last time he was here?

GEORGE Pearl.

PEARL Me feel sorry for the man.

GEORGE He's a friend!

PEARL Listen.
Men fight, know that.
You understand that.
The world doesn't stop.

Beat.

We haven't had any problems here before.
Not having problems tonight.

GEORGE How you know?

PEARL You here.
No one would dare.

GEORGE Can only do so much.

PEARL No one would dare.

Beat.

Not in this house.

Under this roof.

This your house.

GEORGE Yeah?

PEARL Our house.

Beat.

Right?

Pause.

People are expecting us to open.

Did you get the vegetables?

Beat.

George!

GEORGE Me forgot.

Sorry.

PEARL Told you to write it down.

Beat.

(Are) You here?

GEORGE Me write it down.

I'll go back and get the vegetables.

PEARL I'll do it.

PEARL picks up her purse and takes off her apron.

Watch the stove.

GEORGE (I) Will.

PEARL Could tidy things up as well.

GEORGE Where the girls?

PEARL Put them to bed.

PEARL *exits.*

GEORGE *starts clearing the room.*

Moving furniture to make room.

GEORGE *picks up a doll on the floor.*

A knock at the door.

GEORGE Who is it?

ROBERT Robert Dunne.

Beat.

I'm looking for Mr Brown.
George Brown the boxer.
I was told he lives here.

GEORGE *opens the door.*

GEORGE I'm George Brown.
How can I help you?

ROBERT It's you!

GEORGE Sorry?
Do I know you?

ROBERT You don't know how happy I am to see you!

Beat.

GEORGE Right.
How can I help you?

ROBERT *walks in.*

ROBERT *spots the picture on the wall.*

ROBERT *goes to the picture.*

ROBERT The Kingston bomber.
That's you.

GEORGE That's a long time ago.
You still haven't said why you're here?

ROBERT Sorry.

I got carried away with myself.

I am a big fan of yours.

Beat.

GEORGE Do you want an autograph?

ROBERT Yes, do you think we can do that.

GEORGE Got something to sign?

ROBERT Yes.

ROBERT *takes out a business card from his pocket.*

Anywhere on the back.

GEORGE *signs the card.*

GEORGE *turns the card over.*

GEORGE *reads the card.*

GEORGE A promoter.

ROBERT I've been looking for you for a long time.

I heard you were in Nottingham.

I can't believe I've found you.

GEORGE Me not interested.

Good day to you.

You can see yourself out.

GEORGE *hands the card back to* **ROBERT.**

ROBERT Wait a minute!

Beat.

You haven't heard what I've got to offer.

GEORGE Think we can do something together.

Get me a big fight.

Make me money.

Make us money.

Something like that?

Beat.

ROBERT Yeah.
Something like that.

GEORGE Me don't fight no more.

ROBERT That's why I'm here.

GEORGE Quit.

Beat.

ROBERT Children.

GEORGE What?

ROBERT The doll you are holding.
You got children.

GEORGE Sorry you wasted your time Mr/

ROBERT Dunne.
You haven't wasted my time.

Beat.

A minute, please?

GEORGE My wife soon back.

ROBERT A minute and I'll be gone.
I've come all the way from London to find you.
I'm just asking for a minute of your time.

GEORGE *listens.*

I watched the Thompson fight.
I was just a lad.
You are still my favourite fighter.

Beat.

The crowd weren't on your side.

People wanted you to stop.

You kept standing up.

No one has given Thompson as good a lick as you.

Pause.

You have heart.

That's a fighter!

GEORGE That's not me anymore.

ROBERT That will always be you.

Some people can quit things.

Stand up and walk away.

That's not you.

This thing, you can't quit.

ROBERT *points to* **GEORGE**'s *picture.*

It quits you.

Beat.

People say you should have won against Thompson.

GEORGE I didn't.

ROBERT I know.

I was there.

He beat you down!

GEORGE You've come to insult me.

ROBERT You weren't ready for Thompson.

GEORGE I was ready.

ROBERT How long did you train in the lead up to the fight?

GEORGE Enough!

Pause.

ROBERT You have to want this.

To have the discipline.

That's what you need.

That's what you lack.

You want me to tell you the truth.

GEORGE I almost won.

ROBERT But you didn't.

You weren't managed properly.

That's what I'm saying.

I'm telling you the truth.

I know I can do better.

GEORGE It doesn't matter.

ROBERT It does.

You can still be a champion.

I believe that.

Pause.

I have a fight for you already.

McGrath.

Beat.

GEORGE McGrath from Birmingham?

ROBERT You heard of him?

GEORGE Read about him in paper.

Pause.

I could take McGrath.

ROBERT That's what I said.

GEORGE Got no jab.

ROBERT He's a dummy.

You'd eat him alive.

Beat.

GEORGE I've got nothing to prove.

ROBERT You have everything to gain.
That's what it comes down to.
Money.

Pause.

GEORGE I can't.

ROBERT Can't or won't?

Beat.

What are you hiding from?
A man with your talents.
You come to Nottingham to hide.

GEORGE I'm not hiding from anything.

ROBERT Then take this chance.
Opportunities like this don't come along that often.

Beat.

It breaks my heart to see you like this.
Living like this.

GEORGE Like what?

ROBERT Your walls are peeling off.

GEORGE It's the damp.

ROBERT Fix the damp then.
Buy yourself a new house.

ROBERT *shrugs.*

I don't know.

GEORGE This is my house.

ROBERT Make it a better house then.

GEORGE I think you should go now.
Beat.
Hear me!

ROBERT Your wife.

Children.

Think what you could do for them.

GEORGE Leave my family out of this.

ROBERT All I'm asking is that you think about it.

I'm staying at the Black Boy hotel in town.

GEORGE Wasting your time.

ROBERT Just think about it.

Sleep on it.

Talk to your wife.

I'll come back tomorrow for your answer.

It was a pleasure meeting you Bomber.

ROBERT lingers and takes a look round.

You deserve better.

ROBERT exits.

GEORGE stares at the card.

GEORGE goes over to the photo of him as boxer.

GEORGE holds a boxing stance.

GEORGE throws a jab.

GEORGE takes it off the wall.

GEORGE studies the photo.

PEARL enters carrying a bag with cabbage and carrots.

PEARL Kept an eye on the stove?

GEORGE Nothing's burning.

PEARL We ready.

GEORGE Almost.

PEARL Got to make some coleslaw.

Pause.

What you doing with that photo?

GEORGE Didn't see me like this?
Should have seen me like this.

PEARL Saw you after.

Beat.

Sorry.

GEORGE I could take on the world.
That's what me remember from that photo.

PEARL Still can.

GEORGE Always say the right things.

Pause.

PEARL Where were you earlier?

GEORGE Went shop.

PEARL Go shop all the time.
Never come back that late.

GEORGE Sorry.

PEARL Guests will be arriving soon.

Beat.

GEORGE You think me could ever fight again?

PEARL What?

GEORGE Give it one more go?

PEARL You are playing about, aren't you?

GEORGE Trying to tell/

PEARL You need to get those thoughts out your head.

GEORGE Listen/

PEARL Too old to fight.

GEORGE Still could.

Pause.

PEARL What's this about?

GEORGE Nothing.

PEARL You sure?

A knock from outside.

Who is it?

GUEST Looking for Pearl's place.
Looking to meet some friends.

PEARL Coming darling.

PEARL *to* **GEORGE.**

Clear those toys upstairs.

Beat.

You ready?
The party's about to start!

GEORGE *puts the picture back up on the wall.*
GEORGE *exits with the doll.*
PEARL *opens the door to the* **GUESTS.**

ACT TWO

Later the same night.

"JUMP IN LINE" by Lord Flea and Calypsonians plays.

The party in full swing.

People dancing.

Men in suits.

Women in beautiful floral dresses.

EARNEST's suit is a bit more special.

LINFORD dances with MARY.

GEORGE sells beer.

GUESTS play dominos.

PEARL walks around waiting on the guests.

Bringing food out, collecting, clearing plates.

People drink and eat.

PEARL dances with a few guests.

LINFORD and MARY bump into another couple as they dance.

MARY stumbles towards PEARL's display cabinet.

LINFORD pushes a MALE GUEST.

MALE/FEMALE GUESTS try to ignore the confrontation.

PEARL Watch yourself now.

LINFORD Push my woman for?

MARY I'm alright.

LINFORD Fucking idiot!

PEARL Nobody allowed a foul mouth in me house!
Curse you out myself!

MARY I wasn't looking properly.
　It's my fault.

LINFORD Let me handle this.

MALE GUEST Listen to your woman.

MARY It was a mistake.

LINFORD She invisible?

PEARL Calm now.

MARY It's nothing.

LINFORD Let me handle this!

MARY Don't talk to me like that.

MALE GUEST What you handle little boy?

LINFORD Want to test me?

MARY Calm down.
　It's alright.

EARNEST Let's see him handle something then!

PEARL Earnest!

GEORGE No fighting.
　Both of you know the rules.

EARNEST It's all talk.

GEORGE Earnest!

EARNEST I'm not the one acting a fool!
　If they want to fight, let them.
　Thought the fighting was out there.
　Got ring side seats right here!

　EARNEST *continues to eat.*

　MALE GUEST *pulls out a flick knife.*

MARY He's got a knife!

EARNEST *continues eating.*

Everyone stops.

The room is suspended.

Music plays.

PEARL *to* **MALE GUEST.**

PEARL Listen to me darling.
Don't want to make a stupid mistake.
This what you came for?
Everyone want to have a good time.
That mean everybody in here.
This isn't their problem.
Don't want it to be my problem.
Everybody's problem.
Hear?
Look at me.
Not here.
Never here.
Not in my place.
Want to kill someone.
Go through me first.
Hearing me?

GEORGE Mind what you do next.
Hear?
You in my house.

PEARL Me don't want no blood on me carpet.

GEORGE You need to go.

MALE GUEST *exits.*

EARNEST *continues eating.*

EARNEST Well that was a lot of nothing.

GEORGE Earnest!

PEARL *to* **GUESTS.**

PEARL Sorry about that.
Here to have a good time.
Everything alright now.
Please, enjoy yourselves.

GUESTS *unsure how to react.*

A bit of music.
That's what we need.

GUEST *puts on* **"BOOGIE ON MY MIND"** *by Laurel Aitken.*
PEARL *starts to dance.*
PEARL *encourages* **GUESTS** *to dance.*
GUESTS *relax.*
The party continues.

MARY He could have killed you.

LINFORD Me fine.

MARY I mean it.

LINFORD I'm not going nowhere.

PEARL Why you fighting?

LINFORD He started it.

GEORGE You both in the wrong.

PEARL That boy could have stuck you.

GEORGE You weren't thinking.
Should throw you out.

MARY It won't happen again.
He's sorry.
Aren't you?

LINFORD Yes.
Me doing it for Mary.

MARY For me?

LINFORD To protect you.

MARY I don't want you fighting.

LINFORD Fight for what is mine.

MARY I can take care of myself.

LINFORD Fighting for you.

EARNEST Boy you don't listen!
She say stop!
It's this heat.
Makes people crazy.
Makes people mad.
This heat isn't like the heat back home.

GEORGE Yeah!

EARNEST That heat, warm your skin up.
Like the sun kissing you all over.

GEORGE This heat make you sweat!

PEARL Need to rain.
Cool bad tempers.

EARNEST That's your problem boy.
Think you own anger.
Think you the only person ever been angry.

LINFORD Me not say that.

*The distant sound of sirens coming close and fading
away.*

PEARL Be careful.
Be glad you're in here.

EARNEST *reads the paper.*

PEARL *and* GEORGE *interact with* GUESTS.

...

LINFORD I had it.
  Know that, right?

MARY You're being silly.
  Don't need to take risks.

LINFORD Like it?

Beat.

MARY Should I be impressed?

LINFORD Yes.

MARY Thought you were smarter than that.

  MARY *goes to leave, it could be playful.*

LINFORD Hold up.
  Where you going?

MARY That doesn't impress me.

  LINFORD *grabs* **MARY** *and kisses her passionately.*

LINFORD Feel that?

Beat.

MARY Yeah, I feel that.

LINFORD That's all you got to feel.

MARY Still don't need to act stupid.

LINFORD Come on, baby.
  Me say sorry.
  What?

Pause.

MARY I'm not going to be one of your women.

LINFORD What?

Beat.

  Where's this come from?

MARY One of many.
  I'm not one of them.

LINFORD You're my only woman.
  Know that.

  Beat.

  Got eyes for no one else.
  Believe me, right?

  Pause.

MARY I don't know.

LINFORD What's there to know?
  Me like you.
  You like me, I think.

  Beat.

  Like me, right?

MARY I do.

LINFORD Told your mother yet?

  Pause.

MARY I will.

LINFORD What does that make me?

MARY I need to find the right time.

  Silence.

  Why do you like me?
  Of all the girls here.
  Why me?

LINFORD Your smile nice.
  Eyes.
  Hair.
  Things people like.

MARY Come on, be serious.
     Why do you like me?

Pause.

LINFORD I like the way you look at me.
     Now.
     Like you here.
     Without fear.
     Wanting to fall.
     Look at me like it hurt.

Pause.

     Like the feel of you in me arms.
     How your body feel close to mine.
     Right.
     Shudder at me touch.
     Fall into me chest.
     Kiss me.
     Taking everything.
     With your touch.
     With your lips.
     Looking at you hurts.

Pause.

     I love you.

MARY *and* LINFORD *kiss.*

     ...

     To LINFORD *and* MARY.

EARNEST Cut that out now!
     We all in the room.

GEORGE Leave them be Earnest.
     Not bothering you.

EARNEST Trying to read my paper.

GEORGE What paper?

EARNEST Post.

GEORGE You read it?

EARNEST Read them all.

GEORGE Headlines.
Words.
Can't know a man that way.

LINFORD Don't want us anymore.

PEARL Not all.

LINFORD Seem like that.

GEORGE We have our use.

LINFORD We all poor around here.
White man as well.

EARNEST Not like you.
Boy, you poor!

EARNEST laughs.

GEORGE Earnest!

EARNEST Telling the truth!

PEARL No need to insult people.

EARNEST We all poor.
You still a nigger.
Say it on the door.

PEARL Got to work.
Only way this country works.

LINFORD Work hard enough.

EARNEST Pockets still empty.

GEORGE Drink and smoke too much.

EARNEST I'm an impeccable citizen.
Only the best smoke and drink.

LINFORD This their country.

EARNEST Can't forget your past.

LINFORD We supposed to be the past.

GEORGE Past?

LINFORD Asked us to come here.
Now them don't want us.

PEARL We part of the empire.

GEORGE Take what you can get.

EARNEST Say there is two and a half thousand West Indians
in Nottingham.

GEORGE What else it say?

PEARL Never believe what it says in the paper.

EARNEST Say we getting important visitors.

GEORGE Who?

EARNEST The queen.

PEARL Who?

EARNEST Say right here.

> **EARNEST** *pretends to read the paper.*
>
> The queen is coming to Nottingham.
> Say she want to meet us.
> Thank us for coming to Nottingham.
> Say also she want come into some people's home.
>
> *The other* **GUESTS** *know it's a joke.*
>
> Want to visit members of the community.

PEARL It say that?

EARNEST Say they want people to come forward.

GEORGE You want to meet the queen!

PEARL She never come here.

EARNEST Post don't lie.
It's down here, in black and white.

> **PEARL** *takes the paper from* **EARNEST**.
> **PEARL** *scans the story.*

PEARL Me can't find where it say/

EARNEST She want to meet Earnest as well!

> **EARNEST** *is already killing himself laughing.*
> **PEARL** *realises she's on the receiving end of a joke.*
> **GUESTS** *who have overheard the conversation also laugh.*
> **PEARL** *lets them laugh for a while.*
> **PEARL** *to* **GEORGE**.

PEARL Why are you laughing?

GEORGE Not supposed to laugh?

PEARL You on my side.

GEORGE You think the queen want to meet us?
Who we?

LINFORD Why won't Liz not want to come here?
We not good enough?

GEORGE Why she want to come to a slum for?
She got people to knight.

EARNEST She's not in charge.

GEORGE Don't stop Pearl loving her though.
She her queen.

EARNEST Who *your* queen?

GEORGE One queen around here.

EARNEST Man know the truth.

PEARL Had enough fun?

EARNEST Didn't mean no harm.
It was just a little joke.

PEARL *throws the paper back to* EARNEST.

One thing true though.

Everyone want to meet Earnest.

GEORGE *laughs.*

GEORGE What it really say in your paper?

EARNEST Talk about Michael.
Say, police still looking for the suspect.

LINFORD Everybody know who did it.

PEARL What you hear?

LINFORD It was a couple white boys.

EARNEST Not going to find them.
All look alike.
Hard to find.

LINFORD All blue eyed.

GEORGE Blonde.

EARNEST Pale as milk.
Could do with a bit of colour.

Beat.

GEORGE Seen him.

PEARL When?

GEORGE Earlier.

When I went shop.

PEARL Went to city hospital?

GEORGE Me was going to tell you.

LINFORD What he say?

Tell you who did this to him?

GEORGE No.

EARNEST What can he say?

GEORGE Man cried in my arms.

Grown man crying in my arms.

Pause.

PEARL Does no good talking about this.

Best move on.

That's what's important.

No more of this.

Hear.

Beat.

There's work to do.

PEARL *starts clearing empty bottles and plates into the kitchen.*

LINFORD *to* **EARNEST.**

LINFORD Them looking for people at Raleigh?

MARY You have a job.

EARNEST What do you know about machining?

LINFORD Can learn.

MARY Are you looking for a new job?

LINFORD Think they would take me on?

EARNEST Not my place to say.
   Always looking for good people.

MARY You like your job.

LINFORD Can me say me hate it?

MARY Yes.

LINFORD Chillwell Ordnance depot is not heaven!

EARNEST Wouldn't earn anywhere as much back home.
   Know that.

   Beat.

MARY You can say what you are thinking.
   I want to know you are thinking.

   Beat.

LINFORD London.
   Maybe someone could use me.
   Could use my skills.

MARY You never said.

EARNEST What you know about London?

LINFORD Not made up my mind yet.
   It's something me look at.

MARY Your work's alright.

LINFORD Me was going to talk to you about it.

MARY When?

   Beat.

EARNEST Won't find anything down there.
   Been there.
   Seen it.
   Nothing to be found down there.
   Believe me.

LINFORD Things have changed.

EARNEST Don't believe me?
Ask George.
He knows.
Nothing good down there.
Got yourself something good here.

LINFORD Me have to try.

GEORGE *to* **EARNEST.**

GEORGE He isn't us.
The boy wants more.

LINFORD *to* **MARY.**

LINFORD Don't have to tell you everything.
Not made up my mind yet.

EARNEST We both left.
Always got demons chasing you.
Down in London.

MARY I wouldn't leave my job without telling you.
I wouldn't move without telling you.

LINFORD It's not the same.

MARY We are together.
That means we talk about it.

LINFORD Don't break your back every day.

EARNEST We all break our backs.
In our own ways.

GEORGE He's right.

LINFORD She's a teacher.

PEARL That's a tough job.

MARY It's not easy.

LINFORD Easier carrying metal.

EARNEST Seen Blackboard Jungle.
Nothing easy about that.

GEORGE Where you watch it?

EARNEST At the pictures.

LINFORD It's better.

EARNEST Took me this girl.
Anna.
Pretty white girl.

GEORGE First I've heard of this one.

MARY I work as hard as you.
I'm good at my job.
You're not going to make feel guilty about it.

GEORGE Pearl works day and night.
Makes your night.
Keep you happy.

Pause.

Me know how hard she work.
Up at dawn
Cleaning.
Then she cooks.
Night after night.

LINFORD Me not say Mary doesn't work hard.

GEORGE Be careful how things come out.
This woman.
God knows what she sees in you.
But she's right by your side.
That mean you lucky.
You take that.
Hold onto her.

Appreciate her.

Beat.

LINFORD Why you leave London, Earnest?

EARNEST Wanted a change.

PEARL Owed money.
    Ran away.

EARNEST I was a business man.
    Business men always owe money.

LINFORD You ran away?

EARNEST I wanted something different.

GEORGE Me believe him.

PEARL There's work to be done.

MARY Can I help?

PEARL No need to.
    You a guest.

MARY I'd feel better.
    Please?

PEARL Alright.
    Take this.

PEARL *hands over a plate to* MARY *and they start clearing other plates and bottles.*

...

MARY Thank you.

PEARL For what?

MARY For letting me come here.

PEARL Couldn't stop you if I tried.

MARY You wouldn't.
    You're my friend.

PEARL Must scare your mother to death.

Beat.

Don't know what you see in him?

MARY He's beautiful.

PEARL They all nice.

MARY I love him.
He loves me.

Beat.

Don't look at me like that.
He does!
Like you and George.

PEARL All boys say they love you.

MARY Not him.

...

EARNEST Can I ask a favour?

GEORGE What you need?

EARNEST I'm a bit short this month.
Sent some money home.
Need something to hold me over.

GEORGE Ask Pearl.
You know that.

EARNEST You in charge as well!

GEORGE She holds the purse.

EARNEST I don't like asking her.
She always digs at me.

...

PEARL What you two talking about?

PEARL *hovers protective over her display cabinet with her special crockery.*

MARY *sits back down with* **LINFORD.**

EARNEST *gestures to the record player.*

EARNEST I can fix you a nice system.

Really turn this place up!

PEARL Like it the way it is.

EARNEST Innovation Pearl!

PEARL What you know about innovation?

EARNEST Parties all over now.

Music.

That's how you stay ahead.

PEARL We doing fine.

EARNEST Need to change soon or later.

That's how business grows.

I can get you a good sound system.

GEORGE *tries to stick wallpaper that's peeling back onto the wall.*

PEARL *watches.*

PEARL There's no point!

GEORGE *persists in trying to stick the wallpaper back up.*

There's no point.

It's too damp.

EARNEST Everything else done up real nice.

That's nothing.

I've seen worse.

GEORGE *tries to stick the wallpaper back on again.*

The wallpaper flops back down again.

PEARL Wasting your time.

EARNEST He's not going to listen to you.

PEARL Stubborn.

EARNEST Everything in this country damp.

GEORGE Not everything.
Just this house.

PEARL It's not so bad.

EARNEST Better than most I've seen.
Most I've lived in to be fair.
You've done it up real nice.
Count your blessings.

GEORGE Nothing damp about back home.

EARNEST A lick of paint here and there.

GEORGE Needs more than a lick of paint.

PEARL A little work.
That's what he can't see.

GEORGE Sure miss home right about now.

PEARL Missing things is a luxury.
Got to be practical about things.

EARNEST Miss it.

Beat.

Every day.

GEORGE What you be doing now?

EARNEST Now?

GEORGE If you were back there now?

PEARL He's not.

GEORGE Let the man dream.

PEARL That's not a dream.

A dream's something possible.

What he has, fantasy.

Men always full of fantasies.

GEORGE How you know?

Maybe Earnest wants to go back.

PEARL He's not going anywhere.

GEORGE How you know?

Can't know what the man's thinking.

PEARL What he going to do back there?

GEORGE Earnest always finds a way.

EARNEST Set roots now.

I hate the sea.

Never been so sick in my life.

My boat ride was longer than yours.

GEORGE Me have me window wide open.

Get that cool breeze come in.

Hear the crickets.

Feel the heat of the setting dusty sun.

Smell of the hot sun on the earth.

My soul feels dusty.

Feel good.

Put my record on.

Hold my woman and dance.

PEARL See!

What me say about men and their fantasies?

EARNEST He was bearing his soul.

PEARL He's not being practical.

EARNEST That's why men lie.

He tells you his dream and you shut him down.

How can he be open again?

PEARL He's my husband.

GEORGE Got to go back sometime.

PEARL Money too good to leave.

GEORGE Know people who want to go back.

PEARL What people?

Beat.

Think that before you get here.
Soon as you here.
Change your mind.

GEORGE Everybody not you Pearl.

PEARL It's a new start.

EARNEST Pearl.

PEARL Earnest.

EARNEST You know how much I love your cooking, right?

PEARL What are you after?
Wants something.

EARNEST Judged and sentenced me already?

GEORGE Sussed you out.

PEARL Men flatter when they want something.
You're no different.

GEORGE Got you there.

EARNEST Just saying/

GEORGE She's joking.
Go on in the kitchen.
Get yourself something to eat.
Fix yourself something up.
The man always eating.
Not an ounce on him.

EARNEST *exits into the kitchen.*

PEARL We're running a business.

GEORGE Spends enough money.

PEARL Did he have to ask in a roundabout way?

GEORGE There.
That's what I'm saying.
Knew what the man wanted.
Had to dig it out of him.

PEARL How me supposed to know what's in his head?

GEORGE Say the same thing all the time.
Know what he wants.
Everybody know what he wants.

PEARL Why doesn't he just say so?
Why doesn't he ask for what he wants?
Can't ask a straightforward question.

Beat.

GEORGE Are you alright?

PEARL *stands guard over the display cabinet.*

PEARL Somewhere else you can put this?

GEORGE That's where they always stay.

PEARL Me asked you to move it.
Last week.
Remember asking you.

Beat.

I'm sorry.

GEORGE Cool temper.

PEARL Sorry.

EARNEST *returns eating.*

EARNEST When was the last time you eat off those plates?

PEARL The queen's birthday.

GEORGE That was June.
The official date.
That's when we last ate off those plates.
Her real birthday's in April.
We have to wait till June.

PEARL That's her official birthday.
Celebrate that back home.
Celebrate it together.

LINFORD She has two birthdays?

EARNEST She's the queen.
She do what she want.

GEORGE Got to be the queen to eat off those plates.

PEARL Me got plenty of other plates.

GEORGE Knows she's moving to a new country.
That's what she brings.
Bought little else with her.
That's what she packed.

EARNEST You pack a coat.

GEORGE She had a coat with her.
Nothing more
Except that china.

PEARL This china belonged to my mother.
Some of the plates in the back.
Belonged to her mother.

EARNEST You take good care of that china.

GEORGE Cleans those plates every Sunday.

Takes some old newspapers and cloth.
Dips the newspaper in water and wipe it clean.
Next, she uses the cloth.
After church, of course.

EARNEST Church is important.

PEARL When the last time you went church?

EARNEST Don't need to go church to understand.
I was baptised Anglican.

GEORGE Good manners are bred in church.
That's what he means.

EARNEST A fallacy.

GEORGE A what?

PEARL How did we get on the church?

EARNEST A lie!
Good manners are bred at home.

GEORGE What's church for then?

EARNEST To scare and keep scaring you.

GEORGE Why?

EARNEST To be a good person.
That you don't sleep with your neighbour's wife.
Steal.
That sort of thing.

EARNEST laughs.

GEORGE Pastor Wilson would scare anyone good.

EARNEST Time he's finished with Revelations.
Swear never to sin again!

They laugh.

Is Gayle coming tonight?

GEORGE Why you asking?

EARNEST Usually here now.

GEORGE You sweet on her?

EARNEST Where you hear me say that?

PEARL He's sweet on her.

GEORGE She sweet on him?

EARNEST Who not sweet on me?

PEARL Not my business.

GEORGE He's sweet on many girls.

EARNEST Single man.
Nothing wrong been sweet on girls.
You have Pearl.
It's a man's nature to be sweet on girls.

PEARL But you got to hold her right.

EARNEST I know how to hold a woman right.

GEORGE Never seen you dance.

PEARL He don't know how to hold a woman right.

EARNEST When you see me dance?

PEARL Me seen you sway.
From the corner of my eye.
When the music comes on.
Don't like people see you dance.
Seen you though.
Swaying.

EARNEST They've not seen me dance!

PEARL Me seen you.

EARNEST I can dance!

PEARL George can dance.
  Hold me tight when we dance.

GEORGE Me hold you tight when we dance.

PEARL Sure hold me tight when we dance.
  We haven't danced in a while.

  Beat.

  You want to dance with me now?

GEORGE Not now.

PEARL You sure can dance.
  If I could dance like you I wouldn't stop.
  You'd have to tape my feet to the floor.
  My Kingston Bomber.
  Light on his feet.

GEORGE Me not dancing now.

PEARL You know how to hold a woman right.
  What's that song you like?

GEORGE You agitating for something.

PEARL Come back Liza?
  Or should it be, come back Pearl?
  How does it go?

GEORGE Why you asking?

PEARL George loves this song.
  Say it reminds him of me.
  He sing it to me sometime.

GEORGE People don't need to know that.

PEARL Want you to dance with me.

GEORGE Not going to let it go, are you?

PEARL No.

"COME BACK LIZA" by Harry Belafonte.
GEORGE *dances with* PEARL.
EARNEST *sways in his seat.*
He rolls a joint.
The song ends.

EARNEST Pearl?

PEARL You want now?

EARNEST I'm running a little short/

PEARL What you need money for?
Don't they pay you at work?

EARNEST Pay me.
Make sure they pay me.
Never enough.
Money come in.
Money go out.

PEARL Need to plan your money.

EARNEST Always something to pay for.
You ever seen that?
Leave your house.
Something got to come out your pocket.
Stay in your house.
Something still comes out.
Never stops coming out.

PEARL You smoking.

EARNEST What, this?
It's nothing.

PEARL Always got some fancy suit every time I see you.

GEORGE He look good.

EARNEST That's the point.

PEARL Who are you trying to impress?

EARNEST Me.
  You got to care how you look.

PEARL That's not the point.
  Spending money.

EARNEST What then?

PEARL Don't need to be spending money.

EARNEST Looking good costs money.

  Beat.

PEARL See me at the end of the night.
  We'll sort something.
  As long as you good with the rates.

EARNEST Thank you.
  Need the toilet.

PEARL Don't need to announce it to everybody!

  EARNEST *stands.*

EARNEST Right.

  EARNEST *as he exits he spots a female* GUEST.
  Do I know you, darling?
  Haven't seen you around here before.
  Your first time?

PEARL Leave the poor girl alone.

EARNEST I've done nothing wrong.
  Asking this nice young lady if she know me.
  If she don't.
  Well.
  Earnest!

  EARNEST *extends to shake the* GUEST's *hand.*

GUEST *takes his hand.*

By name

Nature.

And everything else you want.

PEARL *gives* **EARNEST** *a look.*

EARNEST *about to sit.*

PEARL Earnest!

EARNEST Wait for me.
I'll be right back.

EARNEST *exits.*

FEMALE GUEST *moves.*

GEORGE Sit down.
Take a break.
Deserve one.
Need one.

PEARL Me fine.

GEORGE Didn't you say you were tired?
Sit.

PEARL Don't order me about.

GEORGE You're stubborn.
Why you have to always question me?
Sit.

PEARL *sits.*

GEORGE *kneels at her feet.*

GEORGE *goes to massage her feet.*

PEARL We working!

GEORGE Nobody mind.
Let me hold you.

PEARL *laughs.*

...

Nobody mind!

A husband allowed to rub his wife foot.

No law against rubbing your woman's foot.

Nobody mind.

See.

Nobody's looking!

PEARL *lets him massage her feet.*

PEARL Feel tired.

GEORGE There's tension in your foot.

Even your feet tired.

That better?

PEARL Been on my feet all day.

GEORGE *continues to massage* **PEARL***'s feet.*

GEORGE Have to look after your feet.

Most people don't look after their feet.

PEARL Soak them later tonight.

GEORGE Me work them out.

No need to soak them

I've worked them out.

PEARL Like the feel of your hands on me.

GEORGE *massages* **PEARL***'s feet.*

Feel like an old boxer.

GEORGE Yeah?

PEARL Real ragged.

Pause.

I always wondered what it was like.

Sat in that corner.
Your last fight.
Had this faraway look.
Like you were somewhere else.
Like you were not yourself.

Silence.

GEORGE I was scared.

PEARL Scared?

GEORGE Thought nothing else.
Nothing scarier than being hit in the face.
Nothing scarier than that.

PEARL Sometimes that's a good thing.
Make you sure what you want.
Me been thinking as well.

GEORGE I see.

PEARL Been thinking all sorts of things.

GEORGE What you been thinking?

PEARL Me want to open something on the Well's Road.

GEORGE That again.

PEARL We hear each other out.
At the end of the day it's me and you.
Our girls.
Us.
Pearl and George.
Let's talk how we used to.
Can we do that?

Beat.

GEORGE Listening.

PEARL We've saved a little from this.

Business like this, save some more.
Call it Pearl and George's place.
Use those plates.
Make it special.
Make it feel like being home.

PEARL *laughs to herself.*

It's silly, isn't it?

GEORGE Me never think you silly.

PEARL Something official.
Something with a sign above the door.
Legitimate.

GEORGE Me not like you.
Can't talk to people like you.
This.
This all you.

PEARL It's ours.

GEORGE They at ease with you.

PEARL I'm a woman.
They respect you.

GEORGE They respect you.

PEARL They tolerate me.
That's different.

Pause.

Do you think dreams are wasted on people like us?

GEORGE People like us?

PEARL You and me.

GEORGE This was your dream once.

PEARL Things change.

GEORGE How?

> Still us.

Pause.

PEARL Remember when I first saw you fight.

> The smell of blood.
> Noise.
> Crunch.
> Thud of human flesh being pounded.
> Your flesh.
> I was so happy when you stopped.
> Knew you wanted to keep going.
> But I was so happy.
> Hated all the fights.
> Seeing you get hit.
> Stopped.
> Remember what you said to me?

GEORGE What?

PEARL Said now is your time.

> Whatever you want baby.
> It's your time
>
> ...

A knock.

> Time to get back to work.

More urgent knocking.

PEARL *opens the door.*

GAYLE Had me waiting long enough.

PEARL Good evening to you too.

GAYLE You not hear me knock?

PEARL Opened the door.

GEORGE Got the wind up you.

GAYLE Drink.

PEARL You alright?

GAYLE My money is on the table.

PEARL Give her a drink.

> **GAYLE** *drinks a shot.*

GEORGE Steady.

GAYLE Another one.

GEORGE Take it easy.

PEARL The devil's settled upon her.

GAYLE Me money not good enough?

GEORGE Not listening to me.

GAYLE Me not ask you to say anything.
All I want is a drink.

GEORGE She's had enough.

PEARL Give her the drink.

> *Beat.*

GAYLE You not hear her.

PEARL She's alright.

> **GEORGE** *pours the drink.*
> **GAYLE** *drains it.*

GAYLE Where the music?

PEARL Play something.

GAYLE Me want to dance.

PEARL Play something.

> **GAYLE** *approaches* **LINFORD.**

GAYLE Dance with me.

> **LINFORD** *hesitates.*

She doesn't mind.
Do you?

MARY No.
It's a just a dance.

GAYLE Me need a man to hold me now.
My own kind.

LINFORD You drunk.

GAYLE No.
Try loosening yourself.

LINFORD What do you mean by that?

GAYLE Song coming on?
Play the song.

MARY We'll dance later.

GAYLE Play the music.

PEARL Play something.

> *"RUN JOE" by Maya Angelou plays.*
> **GAYLE** *and* **LINFORD** *dance.*
> **GAYLE** *a little too familiar with* **LINFORD**.
> **LINFORD** *stops and pushes* **GAYLE** *off.*

LINFORD What are you doing?

GAYLE Dancing.

LINFORD Touching me all over.

GAYLE That's how we dance.

> **GAYLE** *tries to pull* **LINFORD** *back in.*
> **MARY** *stands up.*

LINFORD Stop now!

GEORGE Cool temper.

PEARL I'll take care of it.

> **EARNEST** *re-enters.*

EARNEST Now, where was I?
Where she gone?

GAYLE What I do?

LINFORD Me don't like the way you dance.
Your hands all over me.

GAYLE You think of me like that?
Black skin to skin.

> **LINFORD** *stops.*
> **GAYLE** *to* **MARY.**

Want to know.

Beat.

All these black men you have.
What makes them come to you?

MARY Because he likes what he sees.

GAYLE What?

GEORGE Enough!

LINFORD We are leaving.

MARY And go where?

LINFORD We'll find somewhere.

MARY I like it here.

LINFORD We'll find somewhere else.

MARY Where we can be ourselves?

LINFORD We'll find somewhere.

Beat.

MARY I don't want to go.

GEORGE Don't need to.

GAYLE You can keep him.
Not worth my time.

GEORGE *to* **PEARL.**

GEORGE Handle this.
You don't have to go.

LINFORD She has to go.
Or else we go.

EARNEST There's no need to start something.

LINFORD Pearl?

PEARL Everyone needs to calm down.

LINFORD *to* **GAYLE.**

LINFORD Need to look at yourself.
Look around.
See who your real friends are.

GAYLE What you saying?

LINFORD If any of us had done what you did.
We'd be out.
Pearl wouldn't stand for none of it.
Would you Pearl?

Pause.

Pearl?
One rule for her.
Another for Mary.
Is that it?

MARY It's fine.

LINFORD No, it's not.

> **LINFORD** *prepares to leave.*
>
> **LINFORD** *to* **MARY.**

Are you coming?

> **LINFORD** *storms out.*

MARY I'm sorry.

> **MARY** *follows and exits.*

PEARL Need to calm yourself.

GAYLE Me calm.
Don't me look calm?
Why people always got to tell me to calm down?
Me not look calm?

Beat.

Me just want to dance.

PEARL Then dance.
Plenty of people to dance with.

EARNEST Let me show you how a real man dances.

> **EARNEST** *approaches to dance with* **GAYLE.**

GAYLE Who say me want you?
Don't come pushing upon me.

EARNEST Was just looking to dance.

GAYLE Didn't say you could push up on me.

EARNEST I'm sorry.

GAYLE Who would want to dance with you?
Look at your raggedy self.
In that clown suit.
Why you think me want you?
Look at yourself!

GEORGE That's it!
    You have to go.

PEARL Come here.
    Stop this silliness.

    PEARL *pulls her away.*

    Play the music.
    I'll take care of it.

    "THE DEVIL" by Lord Melody plays.

    The party continues.

    ...

GEORGE Don't mind her.

EARNEST I'm cool.

    Beat.

    Some chap from London been asking about you?

    Pause.

GEORGE Where you hear that?

EARNEST He find you?

GEORGE You spoke to him?

EARNEST Whispers all over the place.

GEORGE Where you hear that Earnest?

    ...

PEARL What's the matter with you?

GAYLE Me haven't done anything wrong.

PEARL In here you have.
    Those are my guests.
    You're a friend so I gave you a chance.

    ...

EARNEST Say he's a promoter.

    You making a comeback?

GEORGE Grown man like you listening to rumour?

    …

GAYLE Me don't know.

PEARL You were bad to that girl.

    Bad to Earnest to.

GAYLE Didn't mean it.

PEARL You need to apologise.

    Next time you see her.

    Apologise to Earnest as well.

    …

GEORGE This stays between us.

EARNEST Lips are sealed.

    Key thrown away.

GEORGE He offered me a fight.

EARNEST Who?

GEORGE McGrath.

EARNEST You can take McGrath!

GEORGE Says he can make me a champion.

EARNEST What you say?

GEORGE Nothing.

EARNEST Nothing?

GEORGE Men don't come out of nowhere.

    Promise to make you a champion.

EARNEST You tell him no?

GEORGE Not young anymore.

EARNEST Take care of yourself.
　　　Always have done.

GEORGE Always a cost.

　　　...

PEARL You going tell me?

GAYLE Mr Bloom let me go.

　　Pause.

PEARL Why?

GAYLE Say me earning too much.
　　　Work as hard as I can.
　　　Know that.

PEARL Me know.

GAYLE He knows that.
　　　He wouldn't listen.
　　　Me wanted to see Mr Thorne.
　　　He's the real boss.
　　　Wouldn't let me see him.
　　　Mr Thorne wouldn't have let me go.
　　　Made him money.
　　　Made that business money!

PEARL That's no reason to let someone go.

GAYLE Say some of the women complained.
　　　I sew too quick.

PEARL About what?

GAYLE I made too much.
　　　That me earned too much.
　　　Wanted to be paid the same.
　　　Me here to work.

PEARL That's what Mr Bloom say?

GAYLE That's what he say.

PEARL Remember when you came.
Didn't know you.
Told your mother I would look after you.

GAYLE Thank you.

PEARL No need to.

Beat.

It's one day.
One day.
You get up.
Everyone falls!

GAYLE I was pushed!

PEARL That don't matter no more.
Tomorrow you get up.
Go get yourself a new job.
We've all been pushed.

GAYLE But/

PEARL Me won't hear it anymore.
Listen to me.
You hold that anger.
It eats you up.
That anger makes you hate.
Like those women at the factory.
Don't want that.
You know what you're working for.
Working for your mother and father.
That's what you keep in mind.
Understand?

Beat.

GAYLE Yes.

...

PEARL She's calm now.

Got something to say as well.

Beat.

Gayle.

GAYLE I'm sorry George.

This your place.

Me didn't mean no disrespect.

PEARL She's sorry.

GEORGE She has a lot of apologies to make.

GAYLE Sorry, Earnest.

Me didn't mean anything by it.

LINFORD *and* **MARY** *burst in.*

MARY *helps in* **LINFORD.**

LINFORD'*s been in a fight.*

There's blood on his shirt.

GUESTS *stop.*

The party stops.

LINFORD Alright Mary?

GEORGE What happened?

GEORGE *rushes over to help* **LINFORD.**

LINFORD You hurt?

MARY No.

I'm alright.

GEORGE Let me take him.

LINFORD We safe now.

MARY They hurt you.

> **MARY** *starts crying.*
> **LINFORD** *stumbles.*

GEORGE Say what happened?

EARNEST Sit him down.

> **GEORGE** *helps* **LINFORD** *sit.*

GEORGE Take it easy now.

> **LINFORD** *winces.*
> **PEARL** *to* **GUESTS** *trying to calm them down.*

PEARL It's alright.
Nothing to worry about.
You just sit down and enjoy your night.

> *Some* **GUESTS** *leave.*

EARNEST What you go and start now boy?

PEARL We'll have this sorted soon.
Don't let it spoil your night.
Got curried mutton and rice in the back.
Plenty to drink!

> **GUESTS** *unsure.*

Play some music.
Sit down now.
Nothing to worry about.

> ***"MAMA NO WANT NO RICE NO PEAS"*** *by Lord Lebby plays.*

GEORGE Bring him some water.
What happened?

> **GAYLE** *exits to fetch a basin and towel.*

LINFORD We were walking to the pub.
They appeared out of nowhere.

GEORGE Started a fight?

MARY He didn't start anything.

LINFORD I didn't want to fight.

GEORGE Who did this?

EARNEST White boys?

LINFORD Yeah.

MARY We were just walking down the street.

GEORGE They beat the boy.

> **GEORGE** *to* **MARY**.

Where?

PEARL There's no point.
Too many of them.

GEORGE There's a few of us as well!

EARNEST Talking crazy.
You fight all of them?

MARY We tried to leave.

EARNEST Be glad you made it out.
Be thankful about that.

> **GAYLE** *returns with a towel and water in a basin.*
> **MARY** *is shaking.*

GEORGE Get him a shirt.

> **GAYLE** *exits to get a shirt.*

PEARL Come and help him now Mary.
Need to stand by your man now.

EARNEST The girl can't stop shaking.
Let her be.

GEORGE It's the shock.
>Sit down.

>LINFORD *tries to stand up.*
>*Stumbles back down.*

>Don't get up.
>Don't get up!

LINFORD Me alright darling.
>They didn't hurt me.
>This is nothing.
>Made of steel.
>See.

>LINFORD *tries to stand.*
>*He stumbles back down.*

MARY Linford.

EARNEST He'll be fine.

GEORGE We'll take care of him.

PEARL Better have a stomach for this.

EARNEST You take a seat now darling.
>Here.

>GEORGE *to* PEARL.

GEORGE That's not helpful now.
>Always got to push.

>EARNEST *ushers* MARY *into a chair.*

PEARL Me not talking out of turn here.
>Truth.
>This boy all banged up.

GEORGE This is not the time for this.

MARY I'm sorry I...

GEORGE No need to apologise.

PEARL Let me look upon you.
Move away George.
Let me look upon him properly.
Come here Mary.

GEORGE *moves away.*

They bust his face up.

GEORGE You helping or judging him?

MARY *goes to* PEARL *and* GEORGE.

PEARL Let me show you something.
Teach you something.
Need to know this.
Take the towel.
Show you how to clean him up.

MARY *really looks at* LINFORD's *bloody face.*
It shocks her.
PEARL *sees that.*
PEARL *takes over.*
GAYLE *re-enters with a shirt.*

Going to sting.
Going to put some antiseptic on that.
It's going to hurt.

GEORGE Don't talk to him like he's a boy.
He's a man he can handle it.

PEARL *(to* MARY*)* Want to help me?

EARNEST *to* MARY.

EARNEST You want something to drink?
You alright?

MARY *nods.*

Silently crying.

You just cry it out now.

I'll get you some water.

EARNEST *exits to the kitchen.*

PEARL *cleans* **LINFORD**'s *face.*

LINFORD *winces.*

PEARL Don't be a big baby now.

Told you to hold still.

You don't want to get an infection on these.

MARY Be gentle with him.

PEARL You want to do this?

LINFORD Was just defending us.

PEARL *finishes cleaning up* **LINFORD.**

PEARL That's the best me could do.

GEORGE We need to take you to the hospital.

LINFORD Me alright.

GEORGE You need a doctor.

LINFORD They chased us.

Leave it a while.

We'll go later.

GEORGE We'll take him.

EARNEST *returns with a glass of water for* **MARY.**

PEARL *exits with the water and towel and disinfectant.*

LINFORD *changes shirts.*

EARNEST At least you lived.

MARY We didn't do anything wrong.

EARNEST This is not about right or wrong.
  People frightened.
  Frightened people are angry people.
  There's all sorts here now isn't it.
  Change too quick for them.
  Can't stop change though.
  That how it works.

  PEARL returns.

  LINFORD *to* **GEORGE.**

LINFORD Thank you for the shirt.

EARNEST You are not the first.
  Won't be the last.

MARY It wasn't my fault.
  I didn't do anything wrong.

  Beat.

  We didn't do anything wrong!

PEARL When you love somebody.
  You love them with all it brings.

MARY I know that.

PEARL Not the one I'm worried about.

LINFORD Me love her.

PEARL Need more than love in this world.
  Got to have a stomach for this fight.
  Look at his face.
  Stand by your man.
  You frightened at the sight of blood?
  Best get used to it.
  Know about cleaning bloody men.
  Costs more than that.
  Cost more than blood.

MARY I can do it.

PEARL Easy to say.

> When your man came in here busted up you didn't.

LINFORD Don't speak to her like that.

GEORGE Pearl that's enough.

MARY What about if she's right?

> What if it happened again?
> I don't know what I'd do.

> **MARY** *about to leave.*

LINFORD Where are you going?

MARY I can't do this.

LINFORD Do what?

MARY How does this work?

> **LINFORD** *stands.*

LINFORD Listen to me.

> I love you.
> Don't look that bad.
> Listen.
> I'm not scared of them.
> Look at me.
> Say something to me.
> I'm not scared.

> **LINFORD** *heads for the door.*
> **GEORGE** *blocks his path.*

GEORGE Easy now.

EARNEST Didn't knock enough sense into his head.

LINFORD Me not afraid of them.

> **LINFORD** *tries to wrestle past* **GEORGE.**

EARNEST Trying to teach you something and you ignore it.
 Know what I'm talking about.

GEORGE Calm yourself man.

PEARL He's fooling himself.
 Let him go.

> **GEORGE** *restraining him.*
> **GEORGE** *to* **PEARL.**

GEORGE What's got into you?
 That's not helpful.

PEARL Me just want people to face the truth.

LINFORD I'll find every single one of them!

GAYLE Don't be silly now.

MARY Stop!

> *Beat.*

 Stop Linford.
 Come to me.
 Listen to me.
 I'm here.
 You're right.
 Looking at you hurts.
 That scared me before.
 Not now.

PEARL Is it worth this?

GEORGE How can you ask that?
 They love each other.

PEARL You are not looking at things straight.

> **LINFORD** *to* **MARY.**

LINFORD Let's get out of here!

MARY What are you talking about?

It's not safe out there.

LINFORD Not out there.

I mean somewhere else.

Leave.

London.

MARY What about the school?

My class.

PEARL How are you going to survive?

LINFORD We'll survive.

PEARL That sound a lot like dreaming and hoping.

You don't fill a belly with that.

Why do you want to take the girl away from her family?

What about what she wants?

How are you going to take care of her?

LINFORD She can speak for herself.

PEARL She's not saying anything.

She knows this is stupid.

GEORGE Pearl stay out of this.

This not our business.

LINFORD You and me.

We can start again.

Away from all this.

How am I going to show my face tomorrow?

Need to get out.

Me want you to come with me.

Me can't live without you.

MARY You are asking a lot.

LINFORD Just believe in it.

Believe in me.

Please?

Voices off.

A mob building outside.

A thrown bottle smashes through the window.

GUESTS *stop.*

Anxious.

PEARL Don't worry everything alright.

LINFORD I'm ready.

PEARL There won't be any fighting.

LINFORD Me not afraid of them!

EARNEST There's women here.

GAYLE Women can fight too!

> **GUESTS** *ready for fight or flight.*

GEORGE Stay away from the window.

LINFORD Sorry about this.

GEORGE You've nothing to apologise for.

EARNEST Don't go out there.
    Just leave them be.

LINFORD I'm sorry Pearl.

PEARL Don't need to bring attention to ourselves.

GEORGE Lay off the boy.
    He doesn't need the guilt.
    It's not anyone's fault.

    Knock from outside.
    Everybody stops.

    Quiet now.
    Who is it?

    Beat.

SERGEANT WILLIAMS Sergeant Williams.

CONSTABLE REED The police.

Open up now!

GEORGE nervously opens up.

SERGEANT WILLIAMS and CONSTABLE REED enter.

Chuntering among of the GUESTS.

GUEST/S Police!

PEARL Easy now.

SERGEANT WILLIAMS takes off his hat.

SERGEANT WILLIAMS *(to CONSTABLE REED)* Take off your hat.

CONSTABLE REED Why?

SERGEANT WILLIAMS Just do it.

CONSTABLE REED Never take off my hat.

SERGEANT WILLIAMS In this district you do.
This isn't Mapperley.
Remember you are here to help.

CONSTABLE REED reluctant to take off his hat.

Now!

CONSTABLE REED reluctantly takes off his hat.

Good evening Pearl, George/

GEORGE Good evening Sergeant Williams.

PEARL How can we help you Mark?

SERGEANT WILLIAMS We've had reports of a disorder at this
address.

CONSTABLE REED You know it's illegal to have gatherings?

PEARL Nothing wrong with having friends around?

EARNEST We are all friends here.

GAYLE The best of friends.

CONSTABLE REED You know these people Sergeant Williams?

SERGEANT WILLIAMS It's my beat.

CONSTABLE REED The drink.
  Are you selling that?

GEORGE No officer.

CONSTABLE REED Looks like you are.
  I can take you in for that.

PEARL What are we talking about officer?

GEORGE Sergeant Williams?

SERGEANT WILLIAMS Everyone calm down.

> **SERGEANT WILLIAMS** *approaches* **LINFORD.**

  Have you been in a fight tonight boy?

LINFORD Me didn't do anything wrong officer.
  I was defending myself.

SERGEANT WILLIAMS I need you to come with me now.

GEORGE What's he done?

MARY Are you arresting him?

SERGEANT WILLIAMS This is official police business.

GEORGE He didn't do anything wrong.

SERGEANT WILLIAMS Take him.

EARNEST Lets all be sensible now.
  See we can talk about this.
  We can sort this out real nice and easy.

PEARL Officer you know us.
  We're not looking for trouble.
  He's a good boy.
  Have my word on that.

CONSTABLE REED He has to come with us.

PEARL Mark?

SERGEANT WILLIAMS It's just procedure Pearl.

MARY You can't just take him.

CONSTABLE REED Watch me.
    Also mind how you speak to an officer of the law.

MARY Officer please let me explain.
    I didn't mean to disrespect you.
    This man is my boyfriend.
    I can testify to his innocence.
    We were attacked.

CONSTABLE REED Couldn't you find one of your own kind?

MARY What did you say?

CONSTABLE REED You heard me.
    Shouldn't you run off home now.
    Do your parents know you are here?

MARY Yes they do.

PEARL Mark take a seat please.
    George can pour rum for everyone.
    Talk this through.

CONSTABLE REED Are you in charge or not Sergeant Williams?

SERGEANT WILLIAMS You need to come with me now.
    We'll sort this at the station.

    MARY *tries to shield* **LINFORD**.

MARY You can't take him.
    He didn't do anything wrong.

LINFORD It's alright Mary.

MARY Those boys outside started it.

CONSTABLE REED Go home.

MARY I'm not moving.

> **CONSTABLE REED** *brushes* **MARY** *aside.*
>
> **LINFORD** *intervenes.*

LINFORD Get your fucking hands off her!

> **LINFORD** *pushes* **CONSTABLE REED** *off* **MARY**.

CONSTABLE REED Do you see this Sergeant Williams?

> **CONSTABLE REED** *strikes at* **LINFORD** *with his truncheon.*

Don't you ever touch me again!

MARY Leave him alone.

GEORGE Don't have to treat him like that.
He's just looking after the girl.

SERGEANT WILLIAMS Let's all keep our heads now.
We'll take him down to the station.
Mr Brown can come along if he wants.
We'll sort it all out.
If he's innocent like you say.
He'll be back home tomorrow.
I promise.

PEARL Maybe that's best for all.

MARY He's innocent.

PEARL Let the man do his job.

> **LINFORD** *looks to* **GEORGE**.

GEORGE Me right behind you.

MARY I'm coming to the station!

> **LINFORD** *is shoved towards the display cabinet.*

GAYLE Why do you always have to put hands on people?

SERGEANT WILLIAMS Constable Reed!

PEARL Careful now!

> **PEARL** *tries to shield her display cabinet.*
> **PEARL** *pushes* **CONSTABLE REED** *off.*

CONSTABLE REED What did I say about touching filthy wog?

GEORGE Get your hands off me wife!

> **GEORGE** *rushes to protect* **PEARL**.
> **CONSTABLE REED** *strikes out again with his truncheon.*
> **GEORGE** *crashes into the display.*

PEARL No!

> *The display cabinet is smashed including the plates.*
> **CONSTABLE REED** *puts cuffs on* **LINFORD**.

SERGEANT WILLIAMS Are you alright Mr Brown?

PEARL George?

> **SERGEANT WILLIAMS** *offers his hand to* **GEORGE**.
> **GEORGE** *refuses, stands on his own.*

GEORGE Don't need your help.

SERGEANT WILLIAMS Sorry about the plates Mrs Brown.

> **LINFORD** *to* **MARY**.

LINFORD I'll be alright.

Me see you tomorrow.

> **MARY** *to* **LINFORD**.

MARY I believe in you.

> **LINFORD, CONSTABLE REED, SERGEANT WILLIAMS** *exit followed by* **GEORGE**.
> **PEARL, GAYLE, MARY** *and* **EARNEST** *remain.*

GAYLE *comforts* MARY.

PEARL *starts picking up pieces of her plates.*

ACT THREE

Sunday morning.

PEARL *sat over her broken china.*

PEARL *tries to glue broken plates together.*

PEARL *sings the gospel song* **"TAKE MY HAND PRECIOUS LORD".**

Knock from outside.

PEARL *doesn't hear it she continues.*

ROBERT *enters.*

ROBERT *listens.*

PEARL *notices* **ROBERT** *she jumps.*

ROBERT You have a lovely voice.
Sweet like honey.

PEARL *startled.*

PEARL What are you doing?

ROBERT I didn't mean to frighten you.

PEARL What you want?
You a reporter?

ROBERT Robert Dunne.

PEARL My husband upstairs.

ROBERT I'm here to see George.

PEARL Want you to leave.
Lost your mind.
Just walk into strangers homes?

ROBERT George told me to come.

PEARL Don't play with me.

>   *Beat.*

ROBERT I'm not.
>   I'm here to see the Bomber.
>   I'm sorry if I done something wrong.

PEARL What did you say?

ROBERT The Bomber.
>   He's expecting me.

PEARL No one calls him that?

ROBERT That's what I'm here about.

PEARL Who are you?

ROBERT Robert Dunne.

PEARL You said that.
>   What do you want with George?

ROBERT I'm a promoter.
>   I've set him up a fight.

PEARL George doesn't fight anymore.

ROBERT He said/

PEARL Nothing to see George about then.

ROBERT He didn't talk to you/

PEARL He doesn't fight anymore!

ROBERT He said he'd talk to you about/

PEARL You can leave now.

ROBERT Mrs Brown.

PEARL Now!

ROBERT I got him a good match.

PEARL Don't come back here again.

ROBERT There's real money involved.
  A chance at redemption for George.

PEARL Redemption?
  The man don't need redemption!
  He's a good man.

ROBERT A chance to show that a he's great fighter.

PEARL Was a great fighter.

ROBERT I want to hear it from him.

PEARL Got nothing to hear.

  Beat.

  You see those boys outside.
  I'll tell them you are harassing me.
  What happens next is your choice.

  Beat.

ROBERT I'm leaving.

PEARL Never want to see you again.
  Hear?

  ROBERT *about to leave.*

ROBERT Why didn't he tell you?

PEARL Tell me what?

ROBERT That he got a fight.
  George.
  Why didn't he tell you?

PEARL Didn't need to.
  Speak with one voice.

ROBERT That's what you think?

PEARL That's what I know.

ROBERT He wanted the fight.

PEARL He say that?

ROBERT He asked me to come back.

PEARL I think I know my husband Mr Dunne.

ROBERT I don't doubt it.
But your husband is a fighter.
A fighter fights.
You know that, Mrs Brown.

PEARL Think we done.

ROBERT The man is worth something in the ring.

Pause.

PEARL Was down in London when I met George.

Beat.

Met at a party.
All the girls chasing him.
He liked it.
Knew he looked good.
He was famous.
A fighter.
Cocky.
Didn't want any of it.
But he saw me.

Beat.

Me was pretty.
Full.
Ripe.
Men chased me.
George chased me.
Made me care for me.

Beat.

I saw the fight!
Thing about blood.
That makes you...
Stop.
Knocks you back.
Know blood belong in the body.
Not out of it.
Not by choice.

Pause.

I'm the one who patches him up.
When his body's all beat up.
When he winces at my touch.
When he wakes up ashamed.
Ashamed he's lost.
Ashamed he's let his family down.
I've got to kiss his burst lips.
Got to make him feel good again.
Like a man.
Like he's worth something.
That he walk with his head held high.

Pause.

Stopped.
People like you took everything from him.
Won't let you take any more!

GEORGE *enters from upstairs.*

GEORGE What's going on in here?

PEARL Robert was just leaving.
Weren't you?

ROBERT I came for your answer.

PEARL You got your answer.

ROBERT *about to exit.*

ROBERT *(to* **GEORGE***)* You've got my card.

ROBERT *exits.*
GEORGE *sits.*

GEORGE Me can explain.

PEARL Nothing to explain.

GEORGE Should have woke me up.

PEARL Looked like you needed the sleep.

GEORGE Don't need extra sleep.

PEARL You going to see Linford?

PEARL *looking out the window.*
Through where the brick smashed through.
A bright red sun shining through.

Will you look at that sun.
How red it is?

Beat.

Just like those oranges you like.

Beat.

Me think it's going to rain.
That's what she say.

Beat.

Should take an umbrella with you.
Don't want to get caught out.

Silence.

We need to fix this window.

GEORGE Girls gone out playing?

PEARL Taken them over the road to Mrs Thomas'.
Pick them up later.

Silence.

Fix you something to eat?
Food left over from last night.

GEORGE Not hungry.

Silence.

PEARL Going to check on Linford?

GEORGE Owe the boy that at least.

Silence.

PEARL Me get new plates.

Pause.

You go on now.
I've got plenty of work to do.
Should have already started the cooking.
We need more drink for later.

GEORGE Me going to see Linford.

PEARL On your way back.
Get some beer.

Beat.

GEORGE Me don't want to.

PEARL We always open.

GEORGE Not tonight.

PEARL We need the money.

GEORGE Don't need the money.

PEARL Didn't think you were stupid.

GEORGE Don't call me that.

PEARL Didn't think you were.

GEORGE Other ways to make money.

PEARL Fighting?

Pause.

Why didn't you tell me about that man?

GEORGE Me don't know him.

PEARL Called you the Bomber.

GEORGE Lots of people call me that.

Pause.

PEARL What did you say?

GEORGE Me done.

PEARL That's not what he say.

GEORGE Me say so.

PEARL Why did he come back?

GEORGE Have to ask him that.

PEARL Asking you.

GEORGE Don't know!
Alright?

Silence.

PEARL We don't lie to each other.

Silence.

George?

GEORGE *explodes.*

GEORGE What you want me to say?

PEARL We made a deal.

> You don't fight anymore.

GEORGE Things change.

PEARL What things.

> It's still us.

> Pearl and George.

GEORGE What about Michael?

PEARL He's not our problem.

GEORGE Linford?

PEARL You heard Sergeant Williams

> He'll be out today.

GEORGE Not as simple as that.

PEARL It is.

> You trying to make it hard.

GEORGE They come into our house.

> Drink out of our glasses.

> Eat off our plates.

> They our problem.

> *Pause.*

> Me would have told you.

PEARL Had plenty chance.

GEORGE When.

PEARL Plenty!

GEORGE Between buying beer and shopping for vegetables?

PEARL You are being silly.

GEORGE Trying to tell you something here.

> You are not listening.

PEARL Me know/

GEORGE That's the problem.

Think you know everything.

How everybody feel.

How I feel.

Beat.

That man.

That promoter.

I could have talked to him.

You talked.

He wasn't here to see you.

That's my business.

PEARL When you fight, it's also mine.

Beat.

Listen.

He want to use you.

When he's got what he wants he'll leave.

Leave you broke and beat.

They all leave.

Leave you with nothing.

GEORGE You use me.

PEARL What?

GEORGE Me can talk about it.

Entertain you guests.

Tell them stories about my fights.

Can do that?

Pause.

PEARL Listen.

What happened last night/

GEORGE Enough!

Beat.

We've lived this dream of yours.

We've tried.

Made me dream.

That's the truth.

Manner as coarse as my knuckles.

All me had in me was the fight.

Took that away.

Vowed to be what you want.

A man you want.

Pause.

Know my place in this world.

Come when I'm told.

Go when I'm told.

That's the way the world worked out for me.

Me learnt me place.

Pause.

Asked me last night if dreams were wasted on us.

People like you and me.

Truth is me don't know.

Right now.

Me feel like...

Like...

PEARL Feel like what?

Pause.

GEORGE We're not opening tonight!

    GEORGE *stands.*

PEARL George.

GEORGE Not going to have police bursting through my door
again!

GEORGE *exits running into* GAYLE.

GAYLE *enters.*

PEARL I'm sorry.

GAYLE It's alright.
Must be tired.

PEARL Something like that.

PEARL *sits.*
She returns to fixing her plates.
GAYLE *sits down also.*

GAYLE Didn't come to church today?

PEARL People ask?

GAYLE Understand.
You are allowed.

Pause.

Can you save anything?

PEARL Trying to.
Not much to be saved.

GAYLE Save what you can.

Pause.

PEARL She cleaned them every/

GAYLE Every Sunday.
I know.
After church.

Silence.

Linford's friends outside.
Say they are looking after you.
Looking after the place.
Waiting for Linford.

Silence.

George gone to get beer?

PEARL Doesn't want to open.

GAYLE Maybe he's right.
Not tonight.

PEARL Not just tonight.
He wants no more of it.

Beat.

GAYLE That what you want?

PEARL Does it matter.

GAYLE Yes, it does.

PEARL George don't want it anymore.

GAYLE He'll come around.

PEARL You didn't see him.
He wants to fight again.

GAYLE He say that?

PEARL Not in so many words.

GAYLE He say that?

PEARL A promoter came for him.

GAYLE Came when I used to live with you.

PEARL It's different.
There is something in him.
Something I see.
Can't understand.

Beat.

GAYLE What are you going to do?

PEARL Me don't know.

GAYLE You always know.

PEARL Not this time.

Pause.

GAYLE It's not the end of the world.

PEARL This is my job.
My life.

GAYLE We can find something together.

PEARL I hate sewing.

GAYLE It's a job.
My job.

PEARL Don't mean any disrespect by it.
I need to work for myself.

GAYLE You do what you need to.
Isn't that what you said?
You start again.
You know why you are here.

PEARL I've got plans.

GAYLE Dreams.
They won't rent you a place on the Well's Road.

PEARL Me staying.

GAYLE This not your world.

PEARL It is.

GAYLE Can't stay forever.

PEARL We all staying.

GAYLE People go back.

PEARL Everyone keep saying this.
How many you seen go back?

GAYLE All the time.

PEARL Who you seen go back?

Beat.

Built something here.

GAYLE What does George want?

Pause.

PEARL He want what me want.
He's my husband.

Beat.

Is it wrong to want more?

GAYLE *sees a friend in need.*
GAYLE *changes her tone and stands.*

GAYLE Time you gather yourself together.
Clean up this mess.
Prepare as you always do.
You open tonight as usual.
Don't stop.

PEARL Look at this place.

GAYLE Me here.
Tell me what needs doing?

PEARL Clean up.
Downstairs and up.
Put the food on the stove.
We need beer for later.

GAYLE We'll sort what we can now.
I'll start cleaning at the top.
You start down here.
George can get the beer later.
Soon sort this place out like before.
Better.
Where you keep them things now?

PEARL Under the sink.

Beat.

Thank you.

GAYLE No need to thank me.
You are my friend.

PEARL You don't have/

GAYLE Hush now.
Done soon.

PEARL Alright.

GAYLE *exits into the kitchen*
PEARL *hovers over the broken plates.*
She continues.
PEARL *starts cleaning.*
A knock.

Who is it?

MAN 1 Got this woman for you Pearl.

PEARL What woman?

MAN 1 Say she's your neighbour.

PEARL Let her in.

PEARL *opens the door.*
MRS CLARK *enters.*
PEARL *to* MAN 1.

Told you all to go home.

MRS CLARK Mrs Brown.

PEARL Come in.
Please.
I'm sorry about those boys outside.
Told them to go.

MRS CLARK Thank you.

PEARL Caught me doing some cleaning.

Pause.

MRS CLARK Didn't expect it to look like this?

PEARL Look like what?

MRS CLARK I don't know.

PEARL Like your place.

Beat.

Been meaning to come over.
About last night.

MRS CLARK We heard about the boy taken by the police.

PEARL It was a misunderstanding.

MRS CLARK There was a fight.

PEARL There wasn't a fight.

MRS CLARK They took a boy away for fighting.

PEARL It was a mistake.

MRS CLARK I heard the boy was hurt.

Beat.

You know this boy?

PEARL He's a good boy.
Linford.

Pause.

How can I help you Mrs Clark?

MRS CLARK Mary wants to visit this boy.

PEARL They're friends.

MRS CLARK Just friends?

She's keen to see him.

Pause.

Mary's changed.

She sneaks out.

Coming back late.

We suspected she was seeing a boy.

PEARL She like the boy.

Pause.

MRS CLARK You knew her and this boy were together?

PEARL She didn't tell you?

MRS CLARK No she didn't tell me.

It's something you wish your daughter didn't have to hide.

PEARL From you.

MRS CLARK From her mother.

PEARL You don't approve?

MRS CLARK There is nothing to approve.

Beat.

She cried herself to sleep.

PEARL She loves that boy.

MRS CLARK Love?

PEARL Telling you what I've seen.

MRS CLARK Mary and this boy/

PEARL Linford.

MRS CLARK It can't work.

Do you see what I'm saying?

PEARL No.

I don't see what you are saying.

MRS CLARK She likes you.
>   Speak to her.
>   Tell her to give this boy up.
>   She'll listen to you.

PEARL Can't do that Mrs Clark.

MRS CLARK She'll listen to you.

PEARL Did she listen to you?

MRS CLARK It's different.

PEARL You her mother.
>   She's a grown woman.

MRS CLARK Will you?

PEARL I can't help.

MRS CLARK Can't or won't?

>   *Pause.*

>   Our Mary is naive.

PEARL I understand.

MRS CLARK I don't think you do.

>   *Pause.*

>   You run your parties.
>   We don't say anything.
>   People coming and going.
>   Men.
>   Music.

>   *Pause.*

>   We are good people here.
>   Working people.
>   Yet you choose this.
>   To have these parties.
>   Illegal parties.

Parties people up and down this street don't have.

Pause.

You think the rules don't apply to you.
But they do.

PEARL This is all we got.
Get it.
What I know.
That corner.
This street.
It's ours.
Understand?

Beat.

It's all we got.
Fight for it with our very lives.
Just like you.

MRS CLARK You don't belong here.

Pause.

PEARL Have you had any trouble?

MRS CLARK I have people knocking on my door.
Men I don't know.
Looking for this place.

PEARL I'm sorry about that.

MRS CLARK You do nothing about it.

PEARL I'll try/

MRS CLARK What makes you different?

PEARL Different?

MRS CLARK That you do as you like.
Who are you?
What about us?

Pause.

Mary's got a future.

She's bright.

You know she won a scholarship?

When she were younger.

Pause.

You work hard for your family.

To give them chances.

Chances they are due.

Chances that are their birthright.

Chances that are theirs.

PEARL I take my chances.

MRS CLARK This boy will drag her down.

No one will touch her now.

Beat.

No one will touch her now.

Silence.

This boy.

He cannot be any good for her.

You must see that.

Last night.

Pause.

How many more nights like that?

Pause.

If she's truly your friend.

And she thinks she is.

You'll do this.

PEARL Are you done?

MRS CLARK I'll send her over.
Her father is with her.
He wouldn't set foot in here.

PEARL Why does Mary come here?
Have you thought about that?

MRS CLARK She's young.
Curious.

PEARL She's more than curious.

Pause.

She's different.
Don't know how though.
You can't see how.

MRS CLARK She'll grow out of it.

PEARL Hope she never does.

Beat.

Get out of my house.

MRS CLARK I'll send her over.

PEARL Won't do it.

MRS CLARK I thought we/

PEARL Gave you my answer.

MRS CLARK Give it some thought/

PEARL Get out of my house!

Pause.

MRS CLARK I'll have you thrown out.
I'll complain to the council.
The police.

PEARL Police already know.

MRS CLARK I tell them about the parties.

I tell them about how your guests harass my family.

PEARL Won't believe you.

MRS CLARK I'm from here.

I'm local.

They'll listen to me.

Pause.

I'm pleading from one mother to another.

I'd like to see my daughter get married.

Have children.

Have a life.

PEARL Not with Linford?

MRS CLARK She won't have a life with that boy.

Pause.

I'd do anything for my children.

PEARL So would I.

MRS CLARK Tell her it's over.

Tell her that she can't come back.

MRS CLARK *and* PEARL *look at each other.*

MRS CLARK *exits.*

PEARL *is left her own.*

PEARL *picks up her plate.*

A moment.

MARY *bursts in.*

MARY I'm sorry for last night.

PEARL Wasn't your fault.

MARY I'm going to see Linford.

PEARL George's there now.

MARY *about to leave.*

GAYLE *unseen by* PEARL *and* MARY *in the room.*

He doesn't want to see you.
Linford.

MARY Sorry?

Beat.

PEARL Saw him this morning.
I'm sorry.

MARY What are you talking about?

PEARL I don't want to do this.

MARY Do what?

PEARL He doesn't want you anymore.

MARY When did you see him?

PEARL This morning.
Doesn't think it will work.

MARY I don't believe you.
He has to tell me himself.

MARY *about to leave.*

PEARL Put that boy through enough.

MARY I didn't do anything.

PEARL You did.

MARY I love him.

PEARL That's the problem.
Your love is hurting him.
Taking his future away.

MARY I have to see him.

PEARL Know it's the truth.
  Deep down.

MARY He wants to marry me.

PEARL He's a boy.
  Boys say things.
  Told you that.

MARY He meant it.

PEARL Dreaming.
  He can't dream anymore.
  Need to learn how to survive.

MARY He can work.
  I can work.

PEARL When he's boss see him tomorrow.
  They'll fire him.
  His face all marked up.

MARY We can move to London.

PEARL Police record follow you everywhere.

MARY He did nothing wrong.

PEARL Maybe.
  That doesn't matter now.

MARY I know the truth.
  I know what happened.

PEARL Not everyone's in your corner.

MARY Are you?

PEARL Trying to help.

MARY Are you?

PEARL You're my friend.

  Beat.

MARY Tell me what to do?

Pause.

Pearl?

PEARL Give the boy a chance.
Hasn't got what you got.

MARY Which is?

PEARL You belong here.
This your place.
Your home.
Your family.

MARY You belong here.

PEARL You're white.

MARY Do you hear yourself?
Sound like them.

PEARL Sound like who?

MARY Like my mother.
All of them.
Like I've done something wrong loving this man.

Pause.

You looked so different to me.
Like you were something else.
Seen people like you in street.
Now you were living next door.
You said hello to me.
Like it was normal.
It was as well.
I don't know what I was expecting.
It was nice that you talked to me.
I wanted to know about you.

You and George.

You let me ask you questions.

You answered them.

Told me all about yourself.

Let me into your house.

Your home.

You are my friend.

Please.

Pause.

PEARL I wish it could work.

Between you and Linford.

Looking out for you.

You asked me to look out for you.

MARY Doesn't feel like that.

PEARL For Linford.

Beat.

Do you trust me?

Pause.

MARY He doesn't want me anymore?

PEARL I'm sorry.

MARY *heartbroken.*

Go home.

You are doing what's best for him.

If you love him.

MARY *about to exit.*

PEARL You shouldn't come here anymore.

Makes things difficult.

MARY *exits.*

GAYLE *appears.*

PEARL *is surprised and startled.*

Everyone creep up on me today.

Beat.

How long you been hiding?

GAYLE Long enough.

PEARL Said what needed to be said.

GAYLE Lied to that girl.

PEARL Why didn't you say anything?

GAYLE It's not my place.

PEARL I was being cruel to be kind.

GAYLE Didn't sound like it.
Them love each other.

PEARL Don't doubt that.

GAYLE You should have stayed out of it.

PEARL I had my reasons.

GAYLE Love is a messy business.
Kind of thing you need to stay out of.

PEARL Were you not on that girl last night?
Become her best friend overnight?

Pause.

GAYLE Linford will be angry when he finds out.

PEARL Helping him.

GAYLE Not going to think that.

PEARL Won't allow him back here.

Beat.

GAYLE It's Linford.

PEARL Caused all this mess.

GAYLE Speak like him planned it.

PEARL Leave it now.

GAYLE Allowed to talk my mind.

PEARL Didn't ask you to come.
Don't need your help.

GEORGE enters wearily.

You see him?

GEORGE Wouldn't let me.

PEARL When are they letting him go?

GEORGE sits.

GEORGE Don't know.

PEARL What did they say?

GEORGE Don't know!
Wouldn't tell me anything.

GAYLE Keeping him a bit longer that's all.

Pause.

PEARL Must be hungry now.
Do you want me fix you a plate?

GEORGE Not yet.
Have a beer though.

PEARL Early to be drinking.

GEORGE Alright for you and Sergeant Williams.

GEORGE stands to get the beer.

Get it myself.

PEARL I'll get it.

GEORGE Don't have to question everything I do.

PEARL Cool temper.

GAYLE The man's tired.
He's had a hard morning.
Let him have a beer.

PEARL Just trying to/

GEORGE Don't need you to manage me.
Not a guest.
Me your husband.

PEARL *fetches the beer.*

Thank you.

PEARL What are we going to do?

GEORGE Me don't know anymore.

Beat.

Didn't need to treat us like that last night.
This morning at the station.
Sat there like I had done something wrong.
Wouldn't answer my questions.

PEARL Are you going back?

GEORGE Have to.
Till the boy is out.

Pause.

PEARL Need beer for later.

GEORGE Don't start/

MARY, EARNEST *burst in.*

MARY You lied to me!

PEARL Calm down.

MARY Why did you do that?
You said you were my friend.

GEORGE What's going on?

MARY Ask her?

GEORGE Pearl.
What's she talking about?

MARY Told me Linford said he didn't want me anymore.
I met Earnest on the way.
Told me no one could see him.

GEORGE Pearl?
This true Pearl?

EARNEST She took off.
Soon as she heard.

MARY Why would you do that?

GEORGE Pearl!

GEORGE *punches the table in anger.*

PEARL Had my reasons.

GEORGE That's not good enough.
You tell me now.
Hear?

Pause.

PEARL Mrs Clark threatened us.
Tell the police.
Say we were harassing her.

MARY She wouldn't.

PEARL Ask her.

GEORGE She did what?

PEARL Wanted me to break Mary and Linford up.

MARY You should have told me the truth.

PEARL Did what me had to. Me was looking out/

MARY Tell yourself what you need to make yourself feel better.

PEARL Me had no choice.
They'd close the shebeen.

GEORGE Enough of this!

PEARL It's not just about this place.
It's also about our reputation.
Won't give us the restaurant on the Well's Road.
You can be sure of that.

GEORGE It's our home.
It's not a pub.
That's what you forget.
This is our children's home.

PEARL Planning for our future.
Our children's future.
Whilst you...
Daydream about fights and belts.
We don't keep secrets from each other.

GEORGE Head in the clouds.

PEARL Yes, you.

Pause.

GEORGE Want to do this now?

PEARL We in it already.
Made that man believe you wanted to fight.

EARNEST Maybe we should leave.

GEORGE Stay.
Got nothing to hide.

PEARL We're in it now.

Pause.

You old.
Nobody tell you that.
I will.
Your body not got the fight anymore.
These men who promise you dreams.
Want to take the last bits out of your body.
When your body can't take it.
How will you work?
When your body all broken down.
How will you provide?

Beat.

This thing we do.
It keeps us going.
Might provide for us.

Beat.

See.
Not the one with his head in the clouds.

GEORGE We're in it now.

GEORGE *picks up one of* **PEARL**'s *special plates.*

PEARL What are you doing?

GEORGE Fixing myself something to eat.

PEARL Don't use that plate.

PEARL *tries to take the plate from* **GEORGE**.

GEORGE What you doing?

PEARL Don't use that plate.
It's/

GEORGE Just a plate!

PEARL My plate.

> *Pause.*

GEORGE Out of my way.

> **GEORGE** *barges past* **PEARL** *into the kitchen.*

PEARL Stop.

EARNEST You treat each other nicely now.
Get a hold of your senses the both of you.

> **GEORGE** *re-enters with a plate of leftover food.*
> **PEARL** *tries to take the plate from* **GEORGE**.

GEORGE Don't push me Pearl!

> **PEARL** *tries to grab the plate.*
> **GEORGE** *pushes* **PEARL** *off.*

EARNEST Stop it.

GEORGE This.
This is what you fight for?
This place.
This dream.

GAYLE We'll leave now.

> *Knock from outside.*

GEORGE Whoever it is.
Go away.

> *Knocking.*

What did I say?

> **GEORGE** *rips the door open.*

SERGEANT WILLIAMS Mr Brown.

GEORGE What are you doing here?

PEARL Can I help you officer?

Come in.

GEORGE Pearl let me/

PEARL Come in officer.

Please.

> SERGEANT WILLIAMS *enters politely.*
> *He takes off his hat.*
> MRS CLARK *follows in.*

GEORGE What are you doing here?

PEARL Whatever she said is not true.

Our friends don't harass her.

GEORGE (*to* MRS CLARK) You threaten my wife.

Threaten my family.

Walk back into my house.

MRS CLARK The sergeant was looking for my daughter.

MARY Go home.

SERGEANT WILLIAMS I'm here to speak to Mary Clark.

MARY What about?

SERGEANT WILLIAMS I'm here about Linford Jones.

MARY Why do you need to talk to me about Linford?

SERGEANT WILLIAMS Is there somewhere where we can talk/

MARY Here's fine.

SERGEANT WILLIAMS I meant private.

MARY When are you letting Linford go?

SERGEANT WILLIAMS I really do insist we talk in private.

MARY Where's Linford?

Pause.

SERGEANT WILLIAMS He put you down as his next of kin.

Pause.

It is with great regret that I have to/

MARY *screams.*

MARY No!

GEORGE Hold her.

SERGEANT WILLIAM I regret to inform you that Linford passed away in custody overnight.

GAYLE What?

SERGEANT WILLIAMS I'm sorry.

> **GEORGE** *squares up to* **SERGEANT WILLIAMS**.

GEORGE Didn't you promise he'd come home today?
He'd be fine?

PEARL George.

GEORGE Promised, didn't you?
Promised.

MARY No!
It must be a mistake.

> **PEARL** *holds* **GEORGE**.

GEORGE Let me go.

PEARL Cool temper.

MARY You must be mistaken.
Not Linford.
He was here last night.
You've got the wrong person.

SERGEANT WILLIAMS I'm sorry.

GEORGE What have you done to him?

*MARY rushes to attack **SERGEANT WILLIAMS**.*

EARNEST Hold her.

*MRS CLARK tries to hold **MARY**.*

MARY Let me go.
Don't touch me.

*MARY breaks free of **MRS CLARK**.*

SERGEANT WILLIAMS On inspection this morning we discovered his body.

Beat.

We found him like that.

*GAYLE holds **MARY**.*

EARNEST Take her out.
Get her out of here.
She needs some air.

*GAYLE tries to drags **MARY** out of the room.*
*MARY to **PEARL**.*

MARY No!
What have you done to him?
You killed him.

Beat.

*MARY to **MRS CLARK**.*

This is what you wanted.

MRS CLARK No, Mary I/

GEORGE Tell me what you did to him?

*PEARL to **MARY**.*

PEARL That's not what me wanted.

Me sorry.

MRS CLARK Let's go home darling.

MARY I need to see him.

> **MARY** *bursts out the room followed by* **MRS CLARKE** *and*
> **GAYLE.**

SERGEANT WILLIAMS I'm sorry.

GEORGE Linford.

No.

Please not him.

Me swear to God me going to kill a man.

EARNEST Why are you here on your own?

Where your boss?

He need to come down.

He need to come down and explain all this.

SERGEANT WILLIAMS I asked to come.

EARNEST How?

That's what me want to know?

SERGEANT WILLIAMS On inspection this morning we discovered
his body.

PEARL Didn't me say that boy was hurt?

Didn't me say he needed the hospital?

SERGEANT WILLIAMS We put him in his cell.

He went to sleep.

GEORGE You want me to believe that?

SERGEANT WILLIAMS That's the truth.

GEORGE Get out of my house.

Now!

Before me do something you regret.

SERGEANT WILLIAMS *heads for the exit.*

SERGEANT WILLIAMS I'm sorry.

SERGEANT WILLIAMS *exits.*

PEARL What do we do now?

EARNEST We'll go to the police station.

GEORGE Me dreaming?

GEORGE *howls like an animal.*

No please. No.

PEARL Me here.

GEORGE *stands.*

What are you doing?

GEORGE Going to kill a man today.

PEARL Who?

GEORGE Someone must be responsible.

PEARL Calm down.

GEORGE I'm going to kill a man today!

PEARL Know you are hurting.
Hurting as well but you need to cool temper.
Earnest?

EARNEST What am I supposed to say to him?
Loved that boy like he was mine.
Feel like killing too.

GEORGE I had forgotten who I was.
What I am.
Me fight Pearl.
You've always know that.
No one backs me into a corner.

Pause.

Do they want to fucking kill me?

Pause.

Hit back.
Hit hard.
Hit to kill.
Right now.
My heart is broken.
Broken for a life half lived.
Me want it back!

Beat.

The boy couldn't defend himself Pearl.
He did nothing wrong.

Beat.

It's him against me.
That's how I see it.
Whoever hits me.
Hit right back.
Harder.

PEARL Please don't do this?

GEORGE *heads for the door.*

GEORGE Let me go Pearl.

GEORGE *opens the door.*
A restless crowd.
The news about LINFORD's *death is filtering out.*

They killed him.
Me going to kill them.

PEARL Who are you going to kill?

A roar from the crowd.

Please George.

Earnest, please reason with him.

EARNEST What can I say?

PEARL This is not who we are.

EARNEST What are you going to do about it?

PEARL George?
Can we talk?

GEORGE What's there to talk about?

PEARL Earnest?

EARNEST Bricks and mortar Pearl.
This is life.
You fight for life.

PEARL You need to stop and think?
George?

GEORGE Going to kill a man.

GEORGE *goes to leave and* PEARL *follows.*

PEARL Coming.

GEORGE You staying here.
Don't want to worry about you.

EARNEST *goes to exit.*

PEARL Wait a minute George.
Talk to me.
It's us.
Remember.
Pearl and George.
I'll give it all up.
We'll start again.

GEORGE Wait outside for me Earnest.

> **EARNEST** *exits.*

PEARL What are you thinking?
    I think I used to know.
    Knew you.
    Intent on something.
    This isn't you anymore.
    Different now.
    You promised.

GEORGE This who I am.

PEARL What happened to turning the other cheek?

GEORGE It's already red and raw!

PEARL Not every fight is yours.

GEORGE This one is mine.
    Always been mine.

> **EARNEST** *returns.*

EARNEST Let's go.

PEARL George!

> **EARNEST** *and* **GEORGE** *exit.*
> **PEARL** *keeps calling out for* **GEORGE**.
> *Fade to black.*

THIS IS NOT THE END